Piano
Lessons
For
Beginners

Contents

Lessons for Beginners Part 1 – Piano Posture: How to Sit at Piano. Fingering.

If you want to learn to play the piano, you're in the right place. You will find free piano lessons here.

First of all, you will learn **how to sit at the piano** (proper piano posture).

Where you put the piano bench and how you position yourself on the bench is a very important part of piano playing. By having the proper posture and position you will be able to reach the entire keyboard and be comfortable while practicing or playing.

Sit tall but not stiff. Your feet should be flat on the floor and your back straight. Your right foot may be slightly forward especially for using your piano pedals. Position yourself forward on the piano bench toward the piano but make sure you're comfortable. You shouldn't have too much thigh on the bench. Position yourself at the center of the piano.

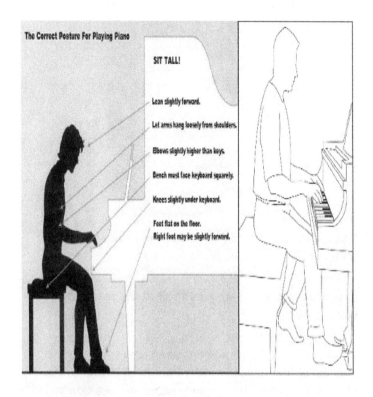

The Correct Posture For Playing Piano

SIT TALL!

Lean slightly forward.

Let arms hang loosely from shoulders.

Elbows slightly higher than keys.

Bench must face keyboard squarely.

Knees slightly under keyboard.

Foot flat on the floor.
Right foot may be slightly forward.

Piano Posture – How to Sit at the Piano

Lean slightly forward. Let your arms hang loosely from your shoulders. Bench must face the keyboard squarely. The bench should be positioned so that your hands are resting over the keys. Elbows should be bent and slightly higher than the keys. Adjust the bench so that your forearms are parallel with the floor. Knees should be slightly under the piano keyboard.

Your fingers should be curved. Pretend you have a bubble in your hand. Be sure to keep your fingernails reasonably short as well.

When it comes to learning to play the piano, I have written an important review that you should read..

Lessons for Beginners – Piano Fingering

Piano Fingering – Guide to Piano Finger Placement

Learn Where Your Fingers Go on the Piano Keyboard

The graphic below illustrates the piano fingering number system. As can be seen, the thumb is the first finger of each hand.

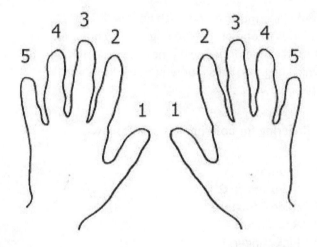

It is very important to learn finger numbers because as part of your beginner piano lessons, you have to learn the proper fingering for scales, chords, arpeggios and musical passages. By using the correct fingers for the correct keys, playing the piano will be easier. You will be able to execute new techniques, master awkward positions, and exercise speed and flexibility. It is important to get this right from the start. There are too many piano players struggling with their playing because they use the wrong fingers for particular keys.

Right hand piano fingerings for Beethoven's Ode To Joy.

Fingered piano music marks each note with a number that corresponds to one of the five fingers. The numbers 1-5 are written above or below the notes. These numbers tell you which finger to press for which key. Here's an example below.

Piano fingering for both hands are as follows:

- Thumb: 1
- Index finger: 2
- Middle finger: 3
- Ring finger: 4
- Pinky finger: 5

Piano Lessons 2 – Piano Key Note Names. Right Hand C Position.

Online Piano Lessons – piano keyboard keys

In part 2 of our piano lessons we shall first of all learn about the piano keyboard. The keyboard is made up of white keys and black keys. The black keys are arranged in groups of two and three. As you move up the keyboard, the notes sound higher. As you move down the keyboard the notes sound lower.

I have written about piano keyboard keys in a previous article. For now, we will pay particular attention to the white notes. They are A, B, C, D, E, F and G repeated over and over. As can be seen, only the seven letters of the alphabet are used.

Each white key is recognized by its position in or next to a group of black keys. For instance, C's are found before the 2-black-key group, while G's are found between the first two keys of the 3-black-key group.

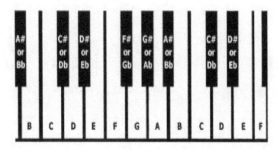

Online Piano Lessons – Piano Keyboard Keys and Right
Hand C Position (Video)

Watch this next video to learn the white notes on a piano,
and the right hand C position. Also, locate middle C on a 61,
76 and 88 key keyboard or piano.

Right Hand C Position

Online Piano Lessons – Right Hand C Position

Do this exercise with me. Place your right number one
finger (your right thumb) on Middle C. Now place your right
number 2 finger (your index finger) on the white note
directly to the right of Middle C. That note is called D. Place
your right middle finger on the note that follow. Next place
your fingers on the other notes, F and G respectively. Make
sure that your fingers are curved and relaxed and your wrist

is up. If done correctly, your hand position should look like the following. This is a right hand C-Position by yours truly.

Now keep each finger on the keys as in the picture above and play the following numbered pattern one finger at a time. 1 2 3 4 5, 1 2 3 4 5, 5 4 3 2 1, 5 4 3 2 1, 1 2 3 4 5, 5 4 3 2 1. Pay attention to fingers 3 and 4; these are known to give beginners a little trouble. Make sure you press the notes one finger at a time and not together.

Piano Lessons – 3 – Quarter, Half and Whole Notes. Bar Lines.

This is part three of our free online piano lessons. In part three we take a look at quarter notes, half notes, whole notes, rhythm, bar lines and measures.

Every note in music has a particular length. Some are long and some are short. We measure the length of these notes by counting.

What is a quarter note? A quarter note (American) or crotchet (British) is a very short note. It is half the length of a half note. It is played for one quarter of the duration of a whole note (or semibreve). Quarter notes are notated with a filled-in oval note head and a straight, flagless stem. The stem usually points upwards if it is below the middle line of the stave or downwards if it is on or above the middle line.

Don't worry if you don't understand many of these terms now. For now, remember that every time you come across a quarter note, count one beat. It takes two quarter notes to make a half note.

The following indicates a quarter note symbol.

Learn how to play piano with the Piano For All piano course.

Next in our free online piano lessons we take a look at the half note. In music, a half note (American) or minim (British) is a note played for half the duration of a whole note (or semibreve) and twice the duration of a quarter note (or crotchet). Half notes are notated with a hollow oval note head (like a whole note) and a straight note stem with no flags. Half notes are drawn with stems to the right of the notehead, facing up, when they are below the middle line of the staff. When they are on or above the middle line, they are drawn with stems on the left of the note head, facing down.

Again, if you're just starting out you may not understand many of these terms. Don't worry they will be clearer as we go along. Just remember that a half note has twice the duration of a quarter note and that you should count two beats every time you come across a half note. Hold the note down and count two beats in your head.

The following indicates a half note symbol.

Watch this lesson:

Learn about quarter notes, half notes, whole notes, rhythm, bar lines and measures.

Learn how to play piano with the Rocket Piano course.

The third type of note in our free online piano lessons is the whole note. A whole note is a very long note. It is twice the length of a half note and four times the length of a quarter note. Every time you come across a whole note, count four beats. In other words, hold the note down on the piano and count four beats. In music, a whole note (American) or semibreve (in the rest of the English-speaking world) is a note represented by a hollow oval note head, like a half note (or minim), and no note stem.

The following indicates a whole note symbol.

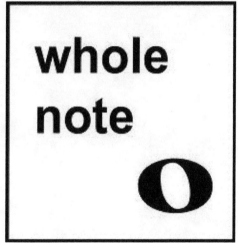

The combination of notes into patterns is called rhythm. Bar lines are the vertical lines on a music staff which divide the staff into measures. The notes and rests between two bar lines on the music staff are known as a measure.

Bar lines and measures

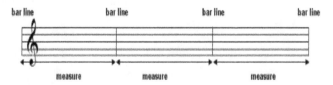

Learn about the eighth note.

Beginner Piano Lessons – 4 – Treble, Bass Clef and Staff. Grand Staff.

Free Beginner piano lessons

Welcome to part four of our free beginner piano lessons. In this lesson we will learn about the grand staff, bass staff, treble staff, bass clef, treble clef and left hand c position.

Treble clef

A symbol indicating that the second line from the bottom of a staff represents the pitch of G above middle C. Also called G clef. This is the most common clef used today, and the only G-clef still in use. For this reason, the terms G-clef and treble clef are often seen as synonymous. It was formerly also known as the "violin clef". The treble clef was historically used to mark a treble, or pre-pubescent, voice part.

Highly Recommended: Click here for the BEST piano/keyboard course I've come across online.

A Treble Clef:

A Treble Staff:

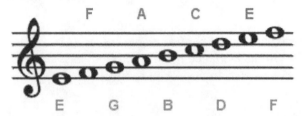

The lines on the treble clef staff correspond to the letters E G B D F, and can be remembered with the help of such phrases as "Every Green Bus Drives Fast", "Every Good Boy Does Fine", "Every Good Boy Deserves Fudge", or "Every Good Band Does Fine". The spaces on the treble clef staff, from bottom to top, correspond to the letters F A C E or "face".

Online Beginner piano lessons:

Reading notes on the Treble Clef and Bass Clef

Bass Clef

A symbol indicating that the fourth line from the bottom of a staff represents the pitch of F below middle C. This is the only F-clef used today, so that the terms "F-clef" and "bass clef" are often regarded as synonymous.

The lines on the bass clef staff (bottom to top) correspond to the notes G B D F A, and can be remembered with the help of the phrase "Good Boys Do Fair Always," or "Good Burritos Don't Fall Apart". The spaces on the bass clef staff correspond (bottom to top) to the notes A C E G.

A Bass Clef:

A Bass Staff:

Free Beginner piano lessons online

Grand staff

The bass staff and treble staff when joined together with a brace make up the grand staff. The treble staff is placed on top of the bass staff. Middle C (C4) occupies the single ledger line between the staves: right in the middle. On piano, the upper staff is normally played with the right hand and the lower staff with the left hand. Staff is more common in American English, stave in British English.

A Grand Staff:

Watch This Lesson: How to Read Piano Notes on the Grand Staff

Left Hand C Position

Next, in our free piano lessons, we talk about the left hand C position on a piano. Place the left hand on the piano keyboard so that the 5th finger falls on the C to the left of middle C. Let the remaining fingers fall naturally on the next white keys. Keep your fingers curved and relaxed. Finger 5 (pinky finger) on C, finger 4 (ring finger) on D, 3 (middle finger) on E, finger 2 (index finger) on F, and finger 1 (thumb) on G.

Now keep each finger on the keys and play the following numbered pattern one finger at a time. 5 4 3 2 1, 5 4 3 2 1, 1 2 3 4 5, 1 2 3 4 5, 5 4 3 2 1, 1 2 3 4 5.

Click here to learn about my top recommendation for learning to play piano. If you want to learn piano the easy way, and not have to endure technical, traditional, boring stuff, I recommend this to you.

Piano Lessons Online Part 5 – Time Signatures. Melodic and Harmonic Intervals.

Welcome to part 5 of our easy piano lessons. In this lesson we take a look at the 4/4 time signature, melodic intervals and harmonic intervals.

Time Signature

The time signature on a musical staff tells you the meter of the music by defining both the number of beats (counts) in a measure and the type of note that fills one beat (count). Most time signatures contain two numbers. The top number tells you how many beats there are in a measure. The bottom number tells you what kind of note gets a beat.

To learn more on this topic and to learn how to read music, check out my course, How To Read Music Fast.

Four Four Time Signature

The most popular time signature is the 4/4 time signature. The following is an example of a 4/4 time signature.

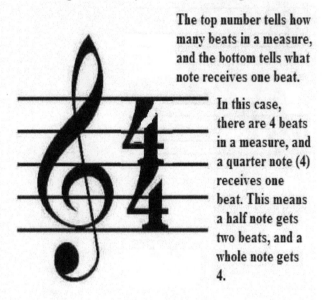

The top number tells how many beats in a measure, and the bottom tells what note receives one beat.

In this case, there are 4 beats in a measure, and a quarter note (4) receives one beat. This means a half note gets two beats, and a whole note gets 4.

In this case there are 4 beats in a measure, and a quarter note receives one beat. This means a half note gets two beats and a whole note gets four.

Four four time is used so much that it is often called common time, written as a bold "C".

Watch this lesson:

A quarter note receives one count, a half note receives two counts and a whole note receives four.

Learn how to play piano with the Piano For All piano course.

Easy Piano Lessons – Intervals

MELODIC INTERVALS

Next in our easy piano lessons for beginners, we take a look at melodic intervals.

The distance between notes is called an interval. When you play notes separately, one after another, you are playing a melody. The distance between these notes is called a melodic interval.

Distances between tones are measured in intervals called 2nds, 3rds, 4ths, 5ths, and so on.

Let us make this much clearer by using the keys on a piano.

The distance from any white key to the next white key, up or down is called a 2nd. On the staff melodic 2nds go from line to space or from space to line.

When you skip a white key, the interval is a 3rd. On the staff, 3rds go from line to line or from space to space.

When you skip two white keys you have a melodic 4th. On the staff melodic 4ths go from line to space or vice versa.

Skip 3 white keys and you've got a melodic 5th. On the staff melodic 5ths go from space to space or from line to line.

For melodic 6ths you skip 4 white keys, melodic 7ths you skip 5 white keys. When you skip 6 white keys you have what is know as an octave.

HARMONIC INTERVALS

Notes played together make harmony. The intervals between these notes are called harmonic intervals. Just like melodic intervals, there are harmonic 2nds, 3rds, 4ths, 5ths, 6ths, etc.

The difference between the two kinds of intervals is melodic intervals are played one note at a time while with harmonic intervals notes are played simultaneously.

Click here for my favorite How to Play Piano course. If you want to learn piano the easy way, and not have to endure technical, traditional, boring stuff, I recommend this to you.

Learn How to Play the Piano – Basic Chords, Time Signatures, Dotted & Tied Notes

Learn Piano – Part One

Welcome to part 6 of our free piano lessons. In this piano lesson we shall take a look at three chords in the key of C, namely, the C major chord, the F major chord and the G major chord. We shall also learn about the 3/4 time signature, and dotted and tied notes. **My Best Recommendation: Click here for the BEST piano/keyboard course I've seen on the Internet.**

A chord is three or more notes played simultaneously. In music theory, a major chord is a chord having a root, a major third, and a perfect fifth. When a chord has these three notes alone, it is called a major triad.

Learn Piano Online – C MAJOR CHORD

The C major chord comprises of three notes, C E and G.

Go to your keyboard or piano and practice playing a C Chord. Be sure that your fingers are nicely curved as mentioned in our first lesson. For the left hand, the 5th finger plays C, the 3rd finger plays E and the 1st finger plays

G. For the right hand, the 1st finger plays C, the 3rd finger plays E and the 5th finger plays G.

Here's an example of a C Major chord on the treble clef in different inversions.

Here's a C Major chord on piano:

Learn Piano Online – F MAJOR CHORD

Let's now take a look at the F major chord. The F major chord comprises of three notes, F, A and C.

The C Major chord is frequently followed by the F major chord and vice versa. Practice going back and forth between the C major chord and the F major chord. For the right hand, the 1st finger plays C in both chords. The 3rd finger moves up to F and the 5th finger moves up to A to form the F chord.

Here's a picture showing the notes of the F chord on piano, starting with the note, C.

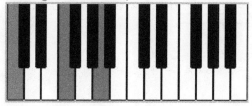

You can also hold the F chord as shown in the diagram below, starting with its root note F, then skipping a key, playing a key (A), skipping a key, playing a key (C) as we did with the C major chord. Finger 1 plays F, finger 3 plays A and finger 5 plays C.

Learn Piano – G MAJOR CHORD

The G major chord comprises of three notes, G, B and D.

Here's a picture showing the notes of the G chord on piano:

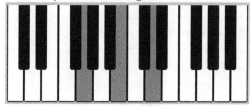

Here's an example of the G chord on the treble clef:

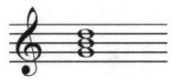

Watch this lesson:

3/4 Time Signature

In piano lesson 5, we talked about time signatures. We saw that the top number in a time signature tells you how many beats there are in a measure (or bar) while the bottom number tells you what kind of note gets a beat.

For a 3/4 time signature there are 3 beats to a measure and a quarter note gets one beat. This means that there can be a maximum of 3 quarter notes in a measure. You can have a half note and a quarter note as well since a half note lasts two beats and a quarter note lasts one beat. You can have any combination of notes as long as they do not exceed three beats.

Dotted notes

A dotted note is a note with a small dot written after it. The dot increases the duration of the basic note by half of its original value. If the basic note lasts 2 beats, the corresponding dotted note lasts 3 beats. So while one would count two beats for a half note, if it is dotted one would have to count three beats. A quarter note gets one beat but a dotted quarter note would last a beat and a half.

Tied notes

A tie is a curved line connecting the heads of two notes of the same pitch, indicating that they are to be played as a single note with a duration equal to the sum of the individual notes' note values.

In some cases one might tie two notes which could be written with a single note value, such as a half note tied to a quarter note (the same length as a dotted half note).

The key is held down for the combined values of both notes.

Tied and dotted notes – Example 1

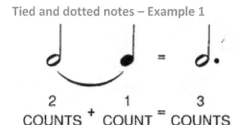

Tied and dotted notes – Example 2

Learn to Play the Piano – Lesson 7 – Music Rests and Note values

In this piano lesson we take a look at rests, note values and time signatures.

Music rests

A rest is an interval of silence in a piece of music, marked by a sign indicating the length of the pause. Each rest symbol corresponds with a particular note value.

My Best Recommendation: Click here for the BEST piano/keyboard course I've seen on the Internet.

Types of music rests

Whole rests and whole notes

A whole note is a musical note that lasts for four beats in 4/4 time. A whole rest is silence equal to a whole note.

The whole rest: a dark rectangle attached to a bar line,

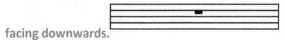

facing downwards.

Half rests and half notes

A half rest is silence equivalent to the value of a half note. It lasts for two beats.

The half rest: a dark rectangle attached to a bar line, facing

upwards.

Quarter rests and quarter notes

A quarter rest is an interval of silence in music that lasts for one beat. Similarly, a quarter note lasts for one beat.

The quarter rest: a squiggly line.

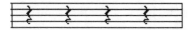

Eighth rests and eight notes

An eight note lasts for half a beat. Likewise, an eight rest lasts for half a beat. It would take two eighth rests to form a rest that lasts for one beat, and similarly, two eight notes to form a quarter note or a note that lasts for one beat.

The eighth rest: a slanted line with a dot.

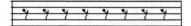

Sixteenth rests and sixteenth notes

A sixteenth note last for a quarter of a beat. A sixteenth rest is a period of silence in music that lasts a quarter of a beat. It takes four sixteenth notes or four sixteenth rests to make one beat.

The sixteenth rest: a slanted line with a double dot.

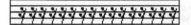

As you learn to play the piano you will realize that there's a lot of simple math involved. As you can see the above is very mathematical.

In a previous piano lesson we looked at quarter, half and whole notes. The following are the images of 8th and 16th notes. They last for half a beat and a quarter of a beat, respectively.

8th notes

An eighth note with stem facing up, an eighth note with stem facing down, and an eighth rest.

Four eighth notes beamed together:

16th notes

A sixteenth note with stem facing up, a sixteenth note with stem facing down, and a sixteenth rest.

Two 16th notes & a 16th rest

Four sixteenth notes beamed together:

Next in our free piano lesson we shall watch a video on time signatures and note values. Enjoy.

Learn to Play Piano – Lesson 8 – Sharp & Flat Signs. Half & Whole Steps. C, F & G Major Keys.

Let's learn to play piano. This is our eighth free piano lesson. In this lesson we take a look at the following:

- The sharp sign
- The flat sign
- Half steps
- Whole steps
- The key of C Major
- Primary chords in C Major
- The C Major Scale
- The Key of F Major
- Primary Chords in F Major
- The F Major Scale
- The key of G Major
- Primary Chords in G Major
- The G Major Scale

Let's learn some music terms and what to do when you come across them.

The sharp sign ♯

The sharp sign (#) before a note means play the next piano key to the right, whether black or white. Sharp means higher pitch and the sharp symbol raises a note by a half tone (semitone). When a sharp appears before a note, it applies to that note for the rest of the measure.

Practice drawing some sharp signs. First draw the two vertical lines. Then add the heavy slanting lines.

The flat sign ♭

The **flat sign** (♭) before a note means play the next piano key to the left, whether white or black. Flat means lower in pitch and the flat symbol lowers a note by a half step. It means lower in pitch by a semitone. When a flat appears before a note, it applies to that note for the rest of the measure.

Practice drawing some flat signs. First draw one vertical line. Then add the heaver curved line.

Learn to play piano online on piano-keyboard-guide.com. Let's talk about half steps and whole steps.

Half steps

A half step is the distance from any key to the very next key above or below (black or white).

What note is a half step lower than G? Answer: G ♭ . What note is a half step higher than F? Answer: F # . F # is the same as G ♭ .

What note is a half step lower than D? Answer: D♭. What note is a half step higher than C? Answer: C♯. C♯ is the same as D♭.

Whole steps

A whole step is equal to two half steps. Skip a key (black or white).

D is one whole step higher than C. And C is one whole step lower than D.

Learn to Play Piano Online – Keys of C, F and G

The Key of C Major

C major (often just C or key of C) is a musical major scale based on C, with pitches C, D, E, F, G, A, and B. Its key signature has no flats/sharps. C major is one of the most commonly used key signatures in music. C major is often thought of as the simplest key, owing to its lack of either sharps or flats. As you learn to play piano you will find that your very first pieces will be very simple ones in this key, and the first scales and arpeggios that you will learn are usually C-major ones.

C major scale fingering

To play a C major scale with the right hand, the fingering is in this ascending order: 1 2 3 – 1 2 3 4 5. In descending order they are 5 4 3 2 1 – 3 2 1. With the left hand the fingers in ascending order are: 5 4 3 2 1 – 3 2 1. And in descending order they are 1 2 3 – 1 2 3 4 5.

An important trick when playing a C major scale is to pass the thumb under the 3rd finger. As soon as the thumb has played the first note (while the 2nd finger is playing the second note) pass the thumb under to the base of the fourth finger, so it will be ready to play its next note in advance.

C Major Scale:

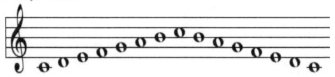

The three most important chords in any key are those built on the 1st, 4th and 5th notes of the scale. Hence the primary chords in the key of C major are C major, F major and G major.

The Key of F Major

F major (or the key of F) is a musical major scale based on F, consisting of the pitches F, G, A, B flat, C, D, and E. Its key signature has one flat (B flat). To play the F major scale with the right hand, the 5th finger is not used.

F major scale fingering

The fingering for the right hand falls into the following groups. 1 2 3 4 – 1 2 3 4 ascending, and 4 3 2 1 – 4 3 2 1 descending. When playing an F major scale with the right hand, in the ascending direction, as soon as finger 1 (the thumb) is played, pass it under finger 4 until it is needed. When descending cross finger 4 over finger 1.

For the left hand the fingering is 5 4 3 2 1 – 3 2 1 ascending, and 1 2 3 – 1 2 3 4 5 descending. When playing an F major scale with the left hand, in the ascending direction, cross finger 3 over finger 1. When descending pass finger 1 under finger 3.

F Major Scale:

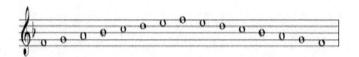

The primary chords in the key of F major are F major, B flat major and C major.

So you want to learn to play piano? Practice makes perfect. Keep practicing your scales.

The Key of G Major

G major (or the key of G) is a major scale based on G, with the pitches G, A, B, C, D, E, and F sharp. Since F is sharp in the G scale, every F will be sharp in the key of G major. Instead of placing a sharp before every F in the entire piece, the sharp is indicated at the beginning in the key signature.

G major scale fingering

Learn to play piano the right way. Proper fingering is important. When playing a G major scale on piano with the right hand, the fingering in ascending order is 1 2 3 – 1 2 3 4 5. When ascending, as soon as the first note of the scale is played, while the second finger plays the second note, pass finger 1 under 3, so it can be ready to play the next note.

In descending order the fingers are 5 4 3 2 1 – 3 2 1. While descending, cross finger 3 over 1 as soon as finger 1 is played.

With the left hand the fingering in ascending order is 5 4 3 2 1 – 3 2 1 and in descending order it's 1 2 3 – 1 2 3 4 5.

G Major Scale

Practice the G major scale with the hands separate. After you've learned it well, you can move on to playing both hands at the same time.

The primary chords in the key of G major are G major, C major and D major.

Practice playing these scales several times daily. Begin slowly and gradually increase speed.

Keyboard Lessons for Beginners 9 – Triads. Minor Scales & Keys. Primary Chords.

Free Keyboard lessons for beginners – part 9.

Welcome to part nine of our beginner lessons. On this page we shall take a look at the following:

- Triads
- Relative minor
- The Key of A minor
- The three kinds of minor scales (natural, harmonic and melodic)
- The A Harmonic Minor Scale

Recommended: Click here for the BEST piano/keyboard course I've come across online.

- Accidentals
- Primary chords in A minor
- The key of D Minor
- The D Harmonic Scale
- Primary chords in D minor

Triads

A triad is a three-note chord consisting of a "root" note together with the third and fifth above it. So in the case of a C chord, the root is C, the third is E and the fifth is G.

Watch this lesson:

Primary triads in the key of C:

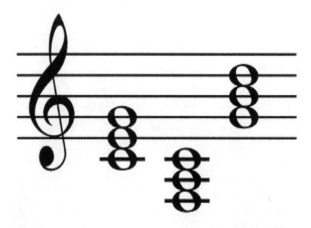

Triads may be built on any note of the scale. Example, C-E-G, D-F-A, E-G-B, F-A-C, G-B-D, A-C-E, and B-D-F. As can be seen, one letter of the alphabet has been skipped between each note. Try out these different root positions and listen carefully to their sound.

In this free keyboard lesson we shall take a look at two different kinds of triad. They are the major triad and minor triad.

A major triad consists of a major 3rd. There are 4 half steps from the root to the 3rd. It consists of a perfect fifth (7 half steps between the root and the fifth). Major triad = root, major 3rd and perfect 5th.

A minor triad consists of a minor 3rd. There are 3 half steps from the root to the 3rd. It also consists of a perfect fifth. Minor triad = root, minor 3rd and perfect 5th. To change from a major triad to a minor triad simply lower the 3rd one half step.

For instance, a C chord is a major triad and consists of the notes C, E and G. A Cm (C minor) chord is a minor triad and consists of the notes C, E ♭ and G.

Types of triads: (For now, check out the first two triads in particular.)

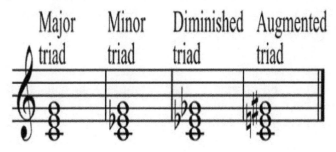

Rocket Piano is one of the best courses I've come across on learning to play keyboard and piano.

The Key of A Minor (Relative of C major) –

The relative minor starts three semitones below its relative major, or the 6th tone; for example, A minor is three semitones below its relative, C Major or on the 6th tone of the scale. The relative minor of a particular major key has the same key signature (no sharps, no flats) but a different root. The relative minor of C is A minor. In the same way, F and D minor are relatives. G and E minor are relatives.

Minor scales

There are three types of minor scales. They are the

- natural minor scale
- harmonic minor scale
- melodic minor scale

The natural minor scale uses only the tones of the relative major scale. Therefore, the A natural minor scale is A B C D E F G. You simply play all the white notes from the sixth of the C major scale.

The harmonic minor scale uses the tones of the major scale except for the 7th tone, G. The 7th tone is raised half a step, ascending and descending. The A harmonic minor scale is A B C D E F G♯.

Accidentals

Since G♯ is not contained in the key signature, it is called an accidental. An accidental is a note whose pitch is not a member of a scale indicated by the most recently applied key signature.

Accidentals – sharp, flat, natural:

The melodic minor scale is separated into two scales, the ascending melodic minor scale and the descending melodic minor scale. In the ascending scale the 6th (F) and 7th (G) are raised a half step. The A ascending minor scale is A B C D E F♯ G♯. The descending melodic minor scale is the same as the natural minor scale.

As part of these free keyboard lessons, practice the three minor scales above until you have learned them well.

The primary chords in A minor are A minor (Am), D minor (Dm) and E major (or E7).

The Key of D Minor

As we said earlier, D minor is the relative of F major. Both keys have the same key signature with one flat, B♭ We've already seen that the relative minor begins on the 6th tone of the major scale.

The D natural minor scale is D E F G A B♭ C

The D harmonic minor scale is D E F G A B♭ C♯

The ascending D melodic minor scale is D E F G A B C# and descending, it's the same as the natural minor scale.

The primary chords in D minor are D minor (Dm), G minor (Gm) and A major or (A7). Practice these chords as part of our beginner keyboard lessons.

Beginner Keyboard Lessons, 10 – Key of Em. E Harmonic Minor Scale. Tetrachords. Chromatic Scale.

Welcome to part 10 of our beginner keyboard lessons. In this lesson we take a look at the following:

- Key of E Minor
- The E Harmonic Scale
- The Primary Chords in E Minor
- Tetrachords
- Key of D Major
- D Major Scale
- Primary Chords in D Major
- The Chromatic Scale

Highly Recommended: Click here for the BEST piano/keyboard course I've come across online.

Key of E Minor

Let's now take a look at the key of E minor (Em).

E minor key (G major) key signature

In the previous lesson we talked about relative minor keys. Let's continue on that note. E minor is the relative of G major. Both keys have the same key signature and consist of one sharp, F♯. The relative minor begins on the 6th tone of the major scale.

Watch this lesson:

The E Natural Minor Scale

The notes of the E natural minor scale are E F♯ G A B C D. Remember that the natural minor uses only notes of the major scale. The only difference is where the scale starts. The scale starts on the 6th tone of the major scale.

The E Harmonic Minor Scale

In a harmonic minor scale the 7th tone is raised by a semitone, ascending and descending. In the case of E minor, D is raised to D♯. Every time this note occurs it is written as an accidental. We've already seen that an accidental is a note that is not contained in the key signature.

So the notes for the E Harmonic minor scale are E F♯ G A B C D♯.

As part of these beginner keyboard lessons, spend time practicing the E harmonic minor scale. What is the fingering for this scale? Let's find out.

The right hand fingering for the E harmonic minor scale is 1 2 3 1 2 3 4 5 ascending, and 5 4 3 2 1 3 2 1 descending.

The left hand fingering for the E harmonic minor scale is 5 4 3 2 1 3 2 1 ascending and 1 2 3 1 2 3 4 5 descending. Practice this scale with hands separately, then together in a contrary motion.

The primary chords in E minor are E minor (Em), A minor (Am) and B7.

Tetrachords

A major tetrachord is a series of four notes, in ascending order, with the following sequence: whole step – whole step – half step. So let's say we start on the note C. One whole step gives us C-D. Another whole step gives us C-D-E. Add a half step and we have C-D-E-F. The notes of a tetrachord must be in alphabetical order.

How about starting on the note, D? If we start on D, a whole step brings us to D-E. Another whole step takes us to D-E-F♯. Add a half step and we've got D-E-F♯-G.

A major scale is made up of two tetrachords joined by a whole step.

To continue our beginner keyboard lessons, let's look at the key of D major.

The D Major Scale

The D major scale is made up of the tetrachord D-E-F♯-G, joined by a whole step that takes us to A. The other tetrachord starts at A and consists of the notes A-B-C♯-D.

D major key signature:

Chromatic Scale (Ascending and Descending):

Next in our beginner keyboard lessons we take a look at the chromatic scale. The chromatic scale (as can be seen above) is made up entirely of half steps. Whether ascending or descending on the keyboard, all black and white notes are used. A chromatic scale can begin on any note.

How to play a chromatic scale (chromatic scale fingering)

Use finger 3 on each black key.

Use finger 1 on each white key except when two white keys are together (E and F, B and C). In that case use fingers 1-2 for the left hand and fingers 2-1 for the right hand.

The left hand fingering for the chromatic scale starting on C is 1 3 1 3 2 1 3 1 3 1 3 2 1, ascending.

The right hand fingering for the chromatic scale starting on C is 1 3 1 3 1 2 3 1 3 1 3 1 2, ascending.

Chromatic scales are a lot of fun. Practice playing them one hand at a time then play both hands together and in contrary motion.

Learn Piano Online – Lesson 11

Learn piano online in our series of lessons.

In this lesson we shall learn about all twelve major keys. First of all let's talk about how one forms a major scale.

We have already looked at the C, F and G major scales. So how does one form any major scale? **My Best Recommendation: Click here for the BEST piano/keyboard course I've seen on the Internet.**

The formula for a major scale is whole-whole-half-whole-whole-whole-half. What does this mean? It means that on your piano keyboard, you move from a whole step, to a whole step, to a half step, to a whole step, to a whole step, to a whole step, and finally to a half step. A whole step is 2 half steps.

Let's take the C major scale for example. To form a C major scale you move from C to D, a whole step. Then from D to E, another whole step. You go from E to F, a half step. Then from F to G, a whole step. G to A is a whole step. A to B is a whole step. Lastly, you move from B to C, a half step.

You can build any major scale using the formula, whole-whole-half-whole-whole-whole-half. You can start on any note and simply follow this formula.

You can learn piano online with our free guide. But for another approach to learning to play the piano I highly recommend the Pianoforall course. **Click here to check out Pianoforall piano lessons.**

practice forming major scales

Using the formula above, practice forming major scales. Start on D and build yourself a major scale. Now start on E. When you're done, start on F. Start on G and build a major scale. Then start on A. Lastly start on the remaining white note, B. The note you start on when building a major scale is known as the root. The root notes you have played so far are C, D, E, F, G, A and B.

Now let's form major scales using the black notes on your piano. Form major scales starting on the notes, C sharp (D flat), D sharp (E flat), F sharp (G flat) and A sharp (B flat).

Learn piano online – keys and key signatures

When a song is written using the scale of C, it is said to be in the key of C. When written using the scale of D, it is said to be in the key of D. And so on,

As you learn to play the various scales you will notice that some keys make use of sharps and flats (black keys). For instance the key of B has 5 sharps. How would a composer indicate that a song is in the key of B? (S)he would use what is known as a key signature. That key signature would show 5 sharps, indicating that there are five sharps in the scale. What this means is that each time the piano player comes across certain notes he would have to play them a semi-tone higher. For instance, instead of playing C, he would play C sharp. Instead of playing D, he would play D sharp. The key of a song is very important to the player. This is one of the first things he must know before starting the song.

Likewise, if the key signature has flats, every time the player comes across certain notes he or she would have to play them a semi-tone lower.

Key Signatures

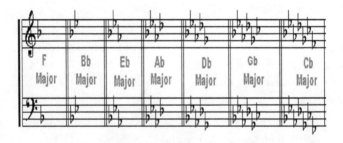

Each key has a certain number of sharps or flats. As you learn piano online, memorize the following.

- In the Key of C, there are 0 sharps and 0 flats.
- In the Key of G, there is 1 sharp.
- In the Key of F, there is 1 flat.

- In the Key of D, there are 2 sharps.
- In the Key of B flat, there are 2 flats.
- In the Key of A, there are 3 sharps.
- In the Key of E flat, there are 3 flats.
- In the Key of E, there are 4 sharps.
- In the Key of A flat, there are 4 flats.
- In the Key of B, there are 5 sharps.
- In the Key of D flat, there are 5 flats.

These are the keys most often used in music.

Other keys include the key of F sharp which has 6 sharps, C sharp which has 7 sharps, and G flat which has 6 flats. But these keys are rarely used outside the world of classical music.

Here's another way of looking at key signatures.

Scales With Sharp Key Signatures

C maj – 0 sharps

G maj – 1 sharp – F#

D maj – 2 sharps – F#, C#

A maj – 3 sharps – F#, C#, G#

E maj – 4 sharps – F#, C#, G#, D#

B maj – 5 sharps – F#, C#, G#, D#, A#

F♯ maj – 6 sharps – F♯, C♯, G♯, D♯, A♯, E♯

C♯ maj – 7 sharps – F♯, C♯, G♯, D♯, A♯, E♯, B♯

Scales With Flat Key Signatures

C maj – 0 flats

F maj – 1 flat – B♭

B♭ maj – 2 flats – B♭, E♭

E♭ maj – 3 flats – B♭, E♭, A♭

A♭ maj – 4 flats – B♭, E♭, A♭, D♭

D♭ maj – 5 flats – B♭, E♭, A♭, D♭, G♭

G♭ maj – 6 flats – B♭, E♭, A♭, D♭, G♭, C♭

C♭ maj – 7 flats – B♭, E♭, A♭, D♭, G♭, C♭, F♭

Free Piano Lessons For Beginners Online – 12

In search of free piano lessons for beginners? This site contains a number of them. In this twelfth online piano lesson we take things to another level. We shall take a look at the following:

Inversion of triads: Triads in all positions

- Root position
- 1st inversion
- 2nd inversion

Highly Recommended: Click here for the BEST piano/keyboard course I've come across online.

Have you checked out our previous free piano lessons? When you have mastered them, you will be ready to proceed to this current one.

We've already looked at triads and how they are formed. A triad is a three-note chord that can be stacked in thirds. A triad consists of the root note, the third and the fifth. There are major and minor triads. For instance, the chord C major is a major triad and is formed with the notes C E G. The chord Am (A minor) is a minor triad and is formed with the notes A C E. In the case of a minor triad, the minor third (in the above example, C) is 3 half steps above the root.

Until now we have only looked at triads in root position. As part of our free piano lessons for beginners let us now look at inversions. We'll start with 1st inversions.

Any root position triad may be inverted by moving the root to the top. So in the case of the chord C, instead of playing C E G, you play the first inversion E G C. All letter names remain the same, but the root is at the top. To play the C chord in root position, you use the fingers 1 3 5. To play it in the first inversion use 1 2 5.

How about the chord, F? In root position you would play F A C. In the 1st inversion, you move the root note, F to the top and play A C F. Between the notes A and C, the interval is a 3rd. Between the notes C and F, the interval is a fourth. Try it now on your piano or keyboard.

What are the notes for the chord Dm (D minor)? The notes are D F A. This is in the root position. To play the 1st inversion of D minor, you play F, A and D. Again, all we've done is simply move the root to the top. The root note is now one octave higher.

How about the minor triad A minor? In the first inversion the notes would be C E A.

As part of your free piano lessons for beginners, practice inverting triads on your piano. Triad inversions are quite interesting!

Here are piano pictures of a C major triad in root position, 1st inversion and 2nd inversion. (I will go through second inversions next.) You can choose different chords and form your own.

C Major Triad

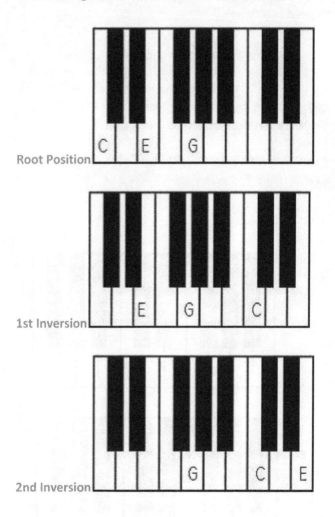

Root Position

1st Inversion

2nd Inversion

As we continue our free piano lessons for beginners, we move to 2nd inversion triads. You can invert the 1st inversion again by moving the lowest note to the top. All letter names remain the same but the root is in the middle.

In the second inversion the root is always the top note of the Interval of a fourth.

Here's an example of the 2nd inversion of a chord on piano. Let's say we have a G chord. In the root position the notes are G B D. In the first inversion the notes would be B D G. In the 2nd inversion the root note, G comes in the middle so the notes are D G B.

Here are piano pictures of an A minor triad in root position, 1st inversion and 2nd inversion.

A Minor Triad

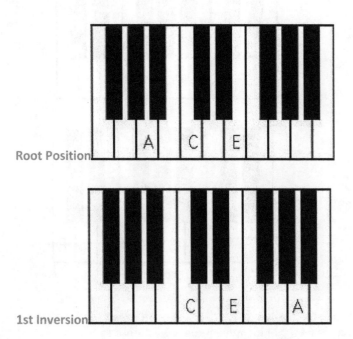

Root Position

1st Inversion

2nd Inversion

Recap

If the root is at the bottom, the triad is in the root position. If the root is at the top the triad is in the 1st inversion. If the root is in the middle, the triad is in the 2nd inversion.

When triads are inverted, major triads remain major; likewise, minor triads remain minor. Practice playing and writing major and minor triads in root position, 1st inversion and 2nd inversion.

Image of C triad in root position, 1st inversion and 2nd inversion

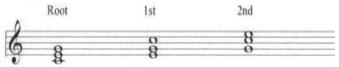

How To Form and Play Piano Scales – Major, Minor, Chromatic, Pentatonic, Blues, Whole Tone & More

Let's learn how to build piano scales.

We shall look at various kinds of scales in this section. We will first of all learn how to build major scales and minor scales. Minor scales include natural or pure minor scales, harmonic minor scales and melodic minor scales. Then we learn how to form chromatic, pentatonic and blues scales and more.

First of all, we need to understand what are half steps and whole steps.

What is a half step? It is the distance from one pitch to the next nearest pitch either up or down. This interval is often called a semitone. For example the distance between C and C sharp on your piano keyboard is a semitone. So is the distance between D and D sharp, E and F, and B and C.

What is a whole step? It is two adjacent half steps. This interval is often called a whole tone. Examples of whole steps are the distance between C and D, D and E, E and F sharp, and B flat and C.

A diatonic scale is a series of eight successive notes that are arranged in a systematic relationship of whole steps and half steps. The eighth note is a duplicate of the first. There are two types of diatonic scales – major and minor scales.

How to Form a Major Scale

Let's learn how to build a major scale.

A major scale consists of eight notes. It is arranged in a pattern of whole steps and half steps. How do you construct a major scale? Simply start with the name of the scale (also known as the root), followed by a whole step, whole step, half step, whole step, whole step, whole step, half step. Let's say you're in the key of C, the notes of the C major scale are C D E F G A B C. C to D is a whole step. D to E is a whole step. E to F is a half step. F to G is a whole step. G to A is a whole step. A to B is a whole step. B to C is a half step.

The formula for forming major scales no matter the key is whole step – whole step – 1/2 step – whole step – whole step – whole step – half step. W-W-H-W-W-W-H

What if we were in the key of G? The notes of the G major scale are G A B C D E F Sharp. Notice how we use F sharp instead of F. In any major scale, there must be a whole step between the 6th and 7th tones of the scale so E had to be followed by a whole step, bringing us to F sharp.

Notes of the C Major Scale:

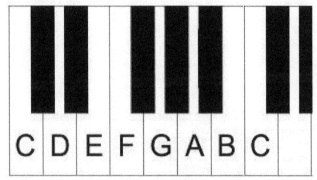

How to Form Minor Piano Scales

Each major key has its relative minor key. The relative minor scale is built upon the sixth tone of the major scale. For instance, the sixth tone in the C major scale is A, therefore the relative minor of C is A minor. C and A minor have the same key signature. In this case, the minor and major scales have the same number of tones. The difference between the major and minor scales is the pattern of the whole steps and half steps.

There are three types of minor scale. They are the pure or natural minor scale, harmonic minor scale and the melodic minor scale. Let's learn how to build these piano scales.

How to Form a Natural or Pure Minor Scale

This scale starts on the sixth degree of its relative major scale. It ascends or descends for one octave using the signature of the major scale. The formula for building a natural minor scale is whole step – half step – whole step – whole step – half step – whole step – whole step. W-H-W-W-H-W-W

As an example, let's take a look at the A natural minor scale. The notes are A B C D E F G A. In a natural (pure) minor scale the half steps occur between 2-3 and 5-6. It can be clearly seen that this scale makes use of the same notes of the relative major scale except for the arrangement of the whole steps and half steps.

Notes of the A minor natural scale:

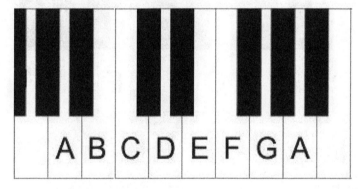

How to Build a Harmonic Minor Scale

Like the natural (pure) minor scale, the harmonic minor scale starts on the sixth degree of its relative major scale. It ascends or descends for one octave using the major scale's key signature, except for the 7th tone which is raised 1/2 a step. For instance, in an A harmonic minor scale, instead of playing G, G sharp is played.

The formula for forming a harmonic minor scale is whole step – half step – whole step – whole step – half step – whole step and a 1/2 step – half step. W-H-W-W-H-W 1/2-H (W 1/2 = whole-step and a half). The half steps occur between 2-3, 5-6 and 7-8, while there's a distance of a step and a half between 6-7.

Example: In an A harmonic minor scale the notes are A B C D E F G# A.

Notes of the A minor harmonic scale:

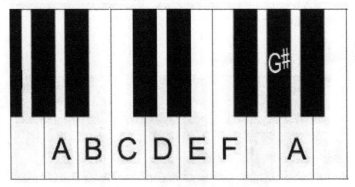

How to Build a Melodic Minor Scale

Next in our lesson on piano scales we take a look at the melodic minor scale. This minor scale also begins on the 6th degree of the relative major scale. It ascends or descends for one octave using the major scale's key signature. However when ascending the 6th and 7th tones are raised half a step. When descending, you simply use the tones of the natural or pure minor scale.

The formula for a melodic minor scale is whole step – half step – whole step – whole step – whole step – whole step –

half step. W-H-W-W-W-W-H The descending formula is the natural minor scale formula backwards. In the melodic minor scale ascending, the half steps occur between 2-3 and 7-8.

Example: In an A melodic minor scale the notes are A B C D E F# G# A (ascending), and A G F E D C B A (descending).

Notes of the A minor melodic scale:

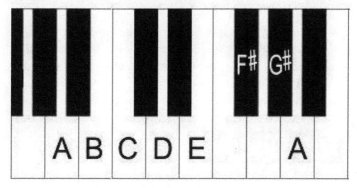

Remember to use the natural minor scale when descending.

Minor Scales: Natural, Harmonic and Melodic

- C Minor Scale
- C Sharp Minor Scale
- D Minor Scale
- E Flat Minor Scale
- E Minor Scale
- F Minor Scale
- F Sharp Minor Scale
- G Minor Scale
- A Flat Minor Scale
- A Minor Scale

- B Flat Minor Scale
- <u>B Minor Scale</u>

How to Build Chromatic Scales

Let's learn how to form chromatic piano scales. This scale is pretty straightforward. You move in half steps. It makes use of accidentals (sharps and flats) depending on whether you are ascending or descending, in connection with the key signature. For the ascending scale you use sharp signs and natural signs, and for the descending scale you use flat signs and natural signs. Chromatic scales have a number of enharmonic tones. Enharmonic tones are tones which are "spelled" differently but sound the same, example C sharp and D flat.

Example: In the key of C, the chromatic scale is C C# D D# E F F# G G# A A# B C (ascending), and C B Bb A Ab G Gb F E Eb D Db C (descending).

Notes of the C chromatic scale:

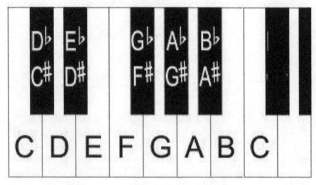

We now know how to form major, natural minor, melodic minor, harmonic minor and chromatic piano scales. Now it's time to practice these scales in different keys. But above all, have fun!

Major Scales

- C Major Scale
- <u>C Sharp Major Scale</u>
- <u>D Major Scale</u>
- E Flat Major Scale
- E Major Scale
- F Major Scale
- F Sharp Major Scale
- G Major Scale
- A Flat Major Scale
- A Major Scale
- <u>B Flat Major Scale</u>
- <u>B Major Scale</u>

More Scales

- Piano Scales in the Key of A and D Minor
- Music Scales in the Key of E Minor and D Major
- <u>Major and Minor Piano Music Scales in All Keys</u>
- Piano Blues Scales
- Pentatonic Scales
- Whole Tone Scale

Highly Recommended: Click here for the BEST piano/keyboard course I've come across online.

How to Play C Major Scale on Piano & Keyboard

Let's learn to play the C major scale on piano (and keyboard). This is the first scale you should learn. Most people start to learn to play the piano with this scale. It is very simple and consists of white keys only.

The C major scale consists of the pitches C, D, E, F, G, A and B. It has no sharp or flat notes and this makes it easy to remember. All you're playing are white keys, so you can't get confused by the black ones.

So how do you play the scale? What fingering is used?

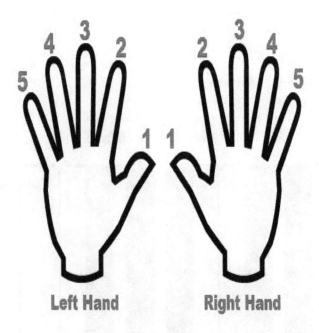

Piano Fingering (Finger Numbers)

Firstly, you need to know the correct numbers for your fingers. For both hands, your thumb is your 1st finger, index finger is 2nd finger, middle finger is 3rd finger, ring finger is 4th finger and pinky finger is 5th finger. This can be seen in the image below.

I made a video showing how to play the C major scale with the right and left hand. Watch it below.

How to Play C Major Scale with Right Hand

Let's start with the right hand. When going up the Cmaj scale, your thumb plays C, 2nd finger plays D and third finger plays E. Then you continue with the thumb which plays F, 2nd finger plays G, 3rd finger plays A, 4th finger plays B and 5th finger plays C. When going up the scale, to play F with your thumb put your thumb under your 3rd finger.

When going down the scale, the same fingers are used. 5th finger plays C, 4th finger plays B, 3rd finger plays A and 2nd finger plays G. Then you continue with your thumb, where the thumb plays F, 3rd finger plays E, 2nd finger plays D and 1st finger plays C. When going down the scale, the 3rd finger goes over your thumb, giving you enough fingers to finish the scale.

Keep practicing this scale until you are very comfortable with it. The more you play it, the better you will get.

C MAJOR SCALE FINGERING

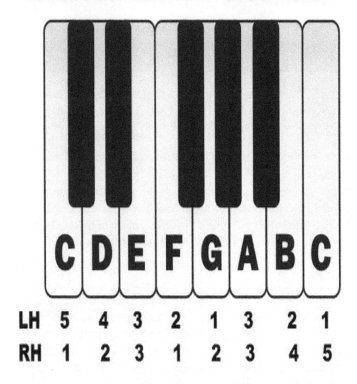

| LH | 5 | 4 | 3 | 2 | 1 | 3 | 2 | 1 |
| RH | 1 | 2 | 3 | 1 | 2 | 3 | 4 | 5 |

How to Play C Major Scale with Left Hand

Left Hand

Let's take this one step further and learn to play the Cmaj scale with the left hand.

For the left hand, when going up the scale, the 5th finger plays C, the 4th finger plays D, the 3rd finger plays E, the 2nd finger plays F and the thumb plays G. The 3rd finger then goes over your thumb and plays A, the 2nd finger plays B and the 1st finger (thumb) plays C.

To go down the scale, the same fingers are used. Therefore, the thumb plays C, the 2nd finger plays B and the 3rd finger plays A. The thumb now goes under the 3rd finger and plays G, the 2nd finger plays F, 3rd finger plays E, 2nd finger plays D and 1st finger plays C.

Major scales contain 7 notes and all use the formula W-W-H-W-W-W-H (whole tone, whole tone, half tone, whole tone, whole tone, whole tone, half tone.) To count a whole tone, count up two piano keys, whether white or black. To count a half tone (or semitone), simply move up by one key. So the distance between C and D is a whole tone, while the distance between E and F is a semitone.

Note Names of the Scale

As can be seen above, the first note of the C major scale is C. It is also called the root of the scale. The 2nd note is D, 3rd note is E, 4th note is F, 5th note is G, 6th note is A, 7th note is B, and 8th note is C.

Scale Degrees

Let's take things a little further. (The most important thing is to be able to play the scale, but let's continue with some music theory.) C is the tonic of this scale. D is the supertonic of the scale. E is the median. F is the subdominant. G is the dominant. A is the submediant. B is the leading tone and C is the octave of the scale.

Here's the C Major Scale on the Treble Clef and Bass Clef, ascending and descending.

C Major Scale Ascending (Treble Clef)

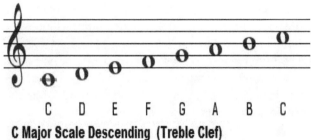

C   D   E   F   G   A   B   C

C Major Scale Descending (Treble Clef)

B   A   G   F   E   D   C

C Major Scale Ascending (Bass Clef)

C D E F G A B C

C Major Scale Descending (Bass Clef)

B A G F E D C

You can play many songs using the notes of this scale only. Many of the popular songs you hear on the radio make use of this simple scale. The chords and harmony also come from that scale.

C Sharp Minor Scale

In this lesson, we will learn how to play the C sharp minor scale. The three types of minor scales are the natural, melodic and harmonic minor scales. We will take a look at all three of them here.

We will learn the notes, intervals and scale degrees of the C sharp minor scale (natural, melodic and harmonic) on the piano, treble and bass clef.

C Sharp Minor Scale

The notes of the C sharp natural minor scale are C#, D#, E, F#, G#, A, and B. This scale has 4 sharps.

Let's take a look at the intervals of the C# minor scale.

1. Tonic – The 1st note of the C-sharp natural minor scale is C#.
2. Major 2nd – The 2nd note of the scale is D#.
3. Minor 3rd – The 3rd note of the scale is E.
4. Perfect 4th – The 4th note of the scale is F#.
5. Perfect 5th – The 5th note of the scale is G#.
6. Minor 6th – The 6th note of the scale is A.
7. Minor 7th – The 7th note of the scale is B.
8. Perfect 8th – The 8th note of the C-sharp natural minor scale is C#.

Here's a diagram of the C sharp minor scale on piano/keyboard.

C# Minor Scale

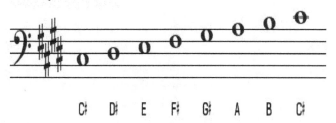

Here's the C sharp natural minor scale on the treble clef.

C sharp minor scale

C♯ D♯ E F♯ G♯ A B C♯

Here's the C sharp natural minor scale on the bass clef.

C sharp minor scale

C♯ D♯ E F♯ G♯ A B C♯

How about the scale degrees? They are as follows:

1. Tonic: C#
2. Supertonic: D#
3. Mediant: E
4. Subdominant: F#
5. Dominant: G#
6. Submediant: A
7. Subtonic: B
8. Octave: C#

There's a formula for forming natural minor scales using whole steps and half steps. That formula is W-H-W-W-H-W-W. "W" stands for whole step and "H" stands for half step.

Let's form the C sharp minor scale with this formula. Of course, our starting note is C#. From C#, we take a whole step to D#. Next, we take a half step to E. From E, a whole step takes us to F#. Another whole step takes us to G#. From G#, we go up a half step to A. From A, a whole step takes us to B. Finally, the last whole step returns us to C#.

The relative major key for the key of C# minor is E major. A natural minor scale/key consists of the same notes as its relative major. The sixth note of the major scale becomes the root note of its relative minor.

Let's now learn the piano fingerings for the C sharp minor scale.

On both the left and right hands, the thumb is finger 1, index finger is finger two, middle finger is finger 3, ring finger is finger 4 and pinky (little) finger is finger 5.

- Notes: C#, D#, E, F#, G#, A, B, C#
- Fingerings (Left Hand): 3, 2, 1, 4, 3, 2, 1, 3
- Fingerings (Right Hand): 3, 4, 1, 2, 3, 1, 2, 3

Triad chords in the key of C sharp minor and their notes:

1. Chord i – C sharp minor. Notes: C# – E – G#
2. Chord iidim – D sharp diminished. Notes: D# – F# – A
3. Chord III – E major. Notes: E – G# – B
4. Chord iv – F sharp minor. Notes: F# – A – C#
5. Chord v – G sharp minor. Notes: G# – B – D#
6. Chord VI – A major. Notes: A – C# – E
7. Chord VII – B major. Notes: B – D# – F#

C Sharp Harmonic Minor Scale

Now that we know the notes of the C sharp minor scale (natural), we now take a look at the C sharp harmonic minor scale.

To play a harmonic minor scale, you simply raise the seventh note of the natural minor scale by a half-step as you go up and down the scale. For example, the notes of the natural C sharp minor scale are C#, D#, E, F#, G#, A, B, C#. To form the C sharp harmonic minor scale, we raise the seventh note by a half step and this results in C#, D#, E, F#, G#, A, B#, C#.

The formula for forming a harmonic minor scale is W-H-W-W-H-W 1/2-H. (Whole step – half step – whole step – whole step – half step – whole step and a 1/2 step – half step.)

Harmonic Minor Scale Intervals

1. Tonic: The 1st note of the C# harmonic minor scale is C#.
2. Major 2nd: The 2nd note of the scale is D#.
3. Minor 3rd: The 3rd note of the scale is E.
4. Perfect 4th: The 4th note of the scale is F#.
5. Perfect 5th: The 5th note of the scale is G#.
6. Minor 6th: The 6th note of the scale is A.
7. Major 7th: The 7th note of the scale is B#.
8. Perfect 8th: The 8th note of the C# harmonic minor scale is C#.

Here's a diagram of the harmonic C sharp minor scale on piano.

C sharp harmonic minor scale

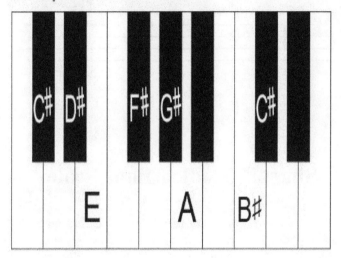

Here's the C# harmonic minor scale on the treble clef.

C sharp harmonic minor scale

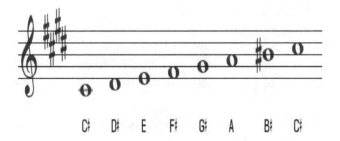

Here's the C# harmonic minor scale on the bass clef.

C sharp harmonic minor scale

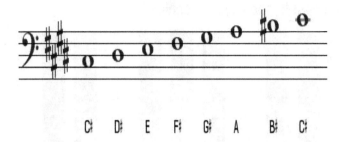

C♯ D♯ E F♯ G♯ A B♯ C♯

C Sharp Melodic Minor Scale

Let's now learn how to form the C sharp melodic minor scale. While the harmonic minor scale raises only the seventh note of the natural minor scale by a half step, the melodic minor scale raises both the sixth and seventh notes by a half step.

The notes of the C sharp natural minor scale (as we've seen) are C♯, D♯, E, F♯, G♯, A, B, C♯. For the C sharp melodic minor scale we raise the 6th and 7th notes by a half step and this results inC♯, D♯, E, F♯, G♯, A♯, B♯, C♯. These notes are used when ascending. When descending, you go back to the natural minor scale.

Notes of the C# melodic minor scale ascending: C♯, D♯, E, F♯, G♯, A♯, B♯, C♯.

Notes of the C# melodic minor scale descending: C♯, D♯, E, F♯, G♯, A, B, C♯. (These are the notes of the C# natural minor scale.)

The formula for a melodic minor scale (ascending) is W-H-W-W-W-W-H. The descending formula is the natural minor scale formula backwards.

Melodic C sharp Minor Scale Intervals

1. Tonic: The 1st note of the C# melodic minor scale is C#.
2. Major 2nd: The 2nd note of the scale is D#.
3. Minor 3rd: The 3rd note of the scale is E.
4. Perfect 4th: The 4th note of the scale is F#.
5. Perfect 5th: The 5th note is G#.
6. Major 6th: The 6th note is A#.
7. Major 7th: The 7th note is B#.
8. Perfect 8th: The 8th note of the C# melodic minor scale is C#.

Here's the C-sharp melodic minor scale on piano, ascending.

C sharp melodic minor scale (ascending)

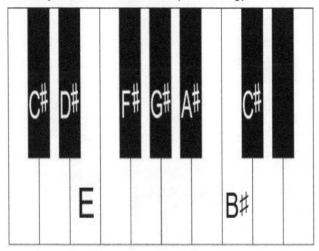

Here's the C sharp melodic minor scale on the treble clef.

C sharp melodic minor scale (ascending)

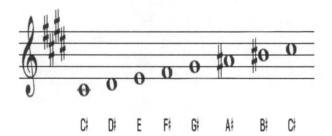

Here's the scale on the bass clef.

C sharp melodic minor scale (ascending)

C♯ D♯ E F♯ G♯ A♯ B♯ C♯

D Minor Scale

This lesson is all about the D minor scale. There are three types of minor scales and we shall take a look at all of them here. They are the natural, melodic and harmonic minor scales.

D Natural Minor Scale

Let's start with the D natural minor scale. This scale consists of the pitches, D, E, F, G, A, B♭, and C. Its key signature consists of one flat.

Note Intervals

1. Tonic: D is the 1st note of the D natural minor scale.
2. Major 2nd: E is the 2nd note of the scale.
3. Minor 3rd: F is the 3rd note of the scale.
4. Perfect 4th: G is the 4th note of the scale.
5. Perfect 5th: A is the 5th note of the scale.
6. Minor 6th: Bb is the 6th note of the scale.
7. Minor 7th: C is the 7th note of the scale.
8. Perfect 8th: D (one octave higher) is the 8th note of the D natural minor scale.

Here's the D minor scale on the treble clef.

Here's the Dm scale on the bass clef.

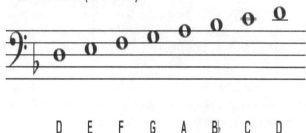

Here's the Dm scale on the piano keyboard.

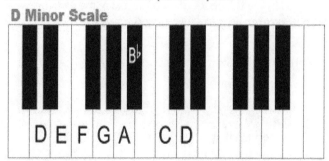

Dm Scale Degrees:

1. Tonic: D
2. Supertonic: E
3. Mediant: F
4. Subdominant: G
5. Dominant: A
6. Submediant: Bb
7. Subtonic: C
8. Octave: D

The relative major key for the key of D minor is F major. A natural minor scale/key consists of the same notes as its relative major. The notes of the F major scale are F, G, A, B♭, C, D and E. As we've seen, the D natural minor uses these same notes, except that the sixth note of the major scale becomes the root note of its relative minor.

The formula for forming a natural (or pure) minor scale is W-H-W-W-H-W-W. "W" stands for whole step and "H" stands for half step. To build a D natural minor scale, starting on D, we take a whole step to E. Next, we take a half step to F. From F, a whole step takes us to G. Another whole step takes us to A. From A, we go up a half step to Bb. From Bb, we take a whole step to C. Lastly, one more whole step returns us to D, one octave higher.

What are the fingerings for the D minor scale? They are as follows:

- Notes: D, E, F, G, A, Bb, C, D
- Fingerings (Left Hand): 5, 4, 3, 2, 1, 3, 2, 1
- Fingerings (Right Hand): 1, 2, 3, 1, 2, 3, 4, 5

Thumb: 1, index finger: 2, middle finger: 3, ring finger: 4 and pinky finger: 5.

Video – How to Play Dm Scale on piano/keyboard:

Let's now take a look at the chords in the key of D minor.

1. Chord i: D minor. Its notes are D – F – A.
2. Chord ii: E diminished. Its notes are E – G – Bb.
3. Chord III: F major. Its notes are F – A – C.
4. Chord iv: G minor. Its notes are G – Bb – D.
5. Chord v: A minor. Its notes are A – C – E.
6. Chord VI: Bb major. Its notes are Bb – D – F.
7. Chord VII: C major. Its notes are C – E – G.

D Harmonic Minor Scale

Let's now take a look at the D harmonic minor scale.

To play a harmonic minor scale, you simply raise the seventh note of the natural minor scale by a half-step as you go up and down the scale. For example:

Natural D Minor Scale = D, E, F, G, A, B ♭ , C, D

Harmonic D Minor Scale = D, E, F, G, A, B ♭ , C#, D

The formula for forming a harmonic minor scale is W-H-W-W-H-W 1/2-H. (Whole step – half step – whole step – whole step – half step – whole step and a 1/2 step – half step.)

Harmonic Minor Scale Intervals

1. Tonic: The 1st note of the D harmonic minor scale is D.
2. Major 2nd: The 2nd note of the scale is E.
3. Minor 3rd: The 3rd note of the scale is F.
4. Perfect 4th: The 4th note of the scale is G.
5. Perfect 5th: The 5th is A.
6. Minor 6th: The 6th note is Bb.
7. Major 7th: The 7th note is C#.
8. Perfect 8th: The 8th note is D.

Here's a diagram of the harmonic D minor scale on piano.

D harmonic minor scale

Here's the scale on the treble clef.

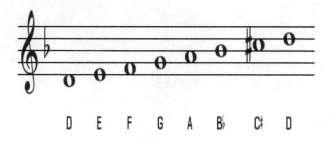

D harmonic minor scale

D   E   F   G   A   B♭   C♯   D

Here's the scale on the bass clef.

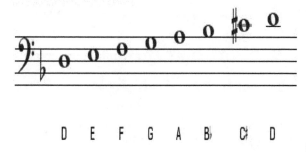

D harmonic minor scale

D   E   F   G   A   B♭   C♯   D

D

harmonic minor scale on bass clef.

D Melodic Minor Scale

For the melodic minor scale, you raise the sixth and seventh notes of a scale by a half step as you go up the scale and then return to the natural minor as you go down the scale.

The notes of the D melodic minor scale ascending are: D, E, F, G, A, B, and C#. The notes of the A melodic minor scale descending are: D, E, F, G, A, Bb, and C (D natural minor scale).

The formula for a melodic minor scale is whole step – half step – whole step – whole step – whole step – whole step – half step. (W-H-W-W-W-W-H) The descending formula is the natural minor scale formula backwards.

Melodic D Minor Scale Intervals

1. Tonic: The 1st note of the D melodic minor scale is D.
2. Major 2nd: The 2nd note of the scale is E.
3. Minor 3rd: The 3rd note of the scale is F.
4. Perfect 4th: The 4th note of the scale is G.
5. Perfect 5th: The 5th note of the scale is A.
6. Major 6th: The 6th note of the scale is B.
7. Major 7th: The 7th note of the scale is C#.
8. Perfect 8th: The 8th note of the scale is D.

Here's a diagram of the melodic D minor scale on piano.

D melodic minor scale (ascending)

Here's the scale on the treble clef.

D melodic minor scale

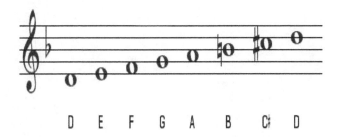

Here's the scale on the bass clef.

D melodic minor scale

D   E   F   G   A   B   C♯   D

Remember that for the melodic minor scale, when descending, you play the natural minor scale.

E Flat Minor Scale

In this lesson, we will learn how to play the E flat minor scale. The three types of minor scales are the natural, melodic and harmonic minor scales. We will take a look at all three of them here.

We will learn the notes, intervals and scale degrees of the E flat minor scale (natural, melodic and harmonic) on the piano, treble and bass clef.

E flat is an enharmonic of D sharp. On piano, the same keys are used to play the two scales. In terms of sound, they are identical. The only difference is the names of the notes. The notes of the D sharp natural minor scale are D♯, E♯, F♯, G♯, A♯, B, and C♯.

E Flat Natural Minor Scale

The notes of the E flat natural minor scale are E♭, F, G♭, A♭, B♭, C♭, and D♭. This scale has 6 flats.

Highly Recommended: Click here for the BEST piano/keyboard course I've come across online.

Let's take a look at the intervals of the Eb minor scale.

1. Tonic – The 1st note of the E-flat natural minor scale is Eb.
2. Major 2nd – The 2nd note of the scale is F.
3. Minor 3rd – The 3rd note of the scale is Gb.
4. Perfect 4th – The 4th note of the scale is Ab.
5. Perfect 5th – The 5th note of the scale is Bb.
6. Minor 6th – The 6th note of the scale is Cb.
7. Minor 7th – The 7th note of the scale is Db.
8. Perfect 8th – The 8th note of the E-flat natural minor scale is Eb.

Here's a diagram of the E flat minor scale on piano/keyboard.

Eb Minor Scale

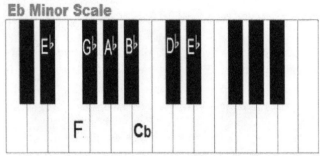

Here's the E flat natural minor scale on the treble clef.

E flat minor scale

Here's the E flat natural minor scale on the bass clef.

E flat minor scale

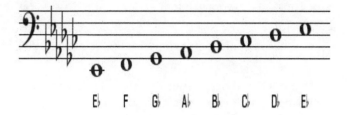

Eb   F   Gb   Ab   Bb   Cb   Db   Eb

How about the scale degrees? They are as follows:

1. Tonic: Eb
2. Supertonic: F
3. Mediant: Gb
4. Subdominant: Ab
5. Dominant: Bb
6. Submediant: Cb
7. Subtonic: Db
8. Octave: Eb

There's a formula for forming natural minor scales using whole steps and half steps. That formula is W-H-W-W-H-W-W. "W" stands for whole step and "H" stands for half step.

Let's form the E flat minor scale with this formula. Of course, our starting note is Eb. From Eb, we take a whole step to F. Next, we take a half step to Gb. From Gb, a whole step takes us to Ab. Another whole step takes us to Bb. From Bb, we go up a half step to Cb. From Cb, a whole step takes us to Db. Finally, the last whole step returns us to Eb.

The relative major key for the key of Eb minor is Gb major. A natural minor scale/key consists of the same notes as its relative major. The sixth note of the major scale becomes the root note of its relative minor.

Let's now learn the piano fingerings for the Eb minor scale.

On both the left and right hands, the thumb is finger 1, index finger is finger two, middle finger is finger 3, ring finger is finger 4 and pinky (little) finger is finger 5.

- Notes of D sharp major scale: D#, E#, F#, G#, A#, B, C#, D#
- Notes of E flat major scale: E♭, F, G♭, A♭, B♭, C♭, D♭, E♭
- Fingerings (Left Hand): 2, 1, 4, 3, 2, 1, 3, 2
- Fingerings (Right Hand): 3, 1, 2, 3, 4, 1, 2, 3

Triad chords in the key of Eb minor and their notes:

1. Chord i – E flat minor. Notes: Eb – Gb – Bb
2. Chord iidim – F diminished. Notes: F – Ab – Cb
3. Chord III – Gb major. Notes: Gb – Bb – Db
4. Chord iv – Ab minor. Notes: Ab – Cb – Eb
5. Chord v – Bb minor. Notes: Bb – Db – F
6. Chord VI – Cb major. Notes: Cb – Eb – Gb
7. Chord VII – Db major. Notes: Db – F – Ab

E Flat Harmonic Minor Scale

Now that we know the notes of the E flat minor scale (natural), we now take a look at the E flat harmonic minor scale.

To play a harmonic minor scale, you simply raise the seventh note of the natural minor scale by a half-step as you go up and down the scale. For example, the notes of the natural E flat minor scale are E♭, F, G♭, A♭, B♭, C♭, D♭, E♭. To form the E flat harmonic minor scale, we raise the seventh note by a half step and this results in E♭, F, G♭, A♭, B♭, C♭, D, E♭.

The formula for forming a harmonic minor scale is W-H-W-W-H-W 1/2-H. (Whole step – half step – whole step – whole step – half step – whole step and a 1/2 step – half step.)

Harmonic Minor Scale Intervals

1. Tonic: The 1st note of the Eb harmonic minor scale is Eb.
2. Major 2nd: The 2nd note of the scale is F.
3. Minor 3rd: The 3rd note of the scale is Gb.
4. Perfect 4th: The 4th note of the scale is Ab.
5. Perfect 5th: The 5th note of the scale is Bb.
6. Minor 6th: The 6th note of the scale is Cb.
7. Major 7th: The 7th note of the scale is D.
8. Perfect 8th: The 8th note of the Eb harmonic minor scale is Eb.

Here's a diagram of the harmonic E flat minor scale on piano.

E flat harmonic minor scale

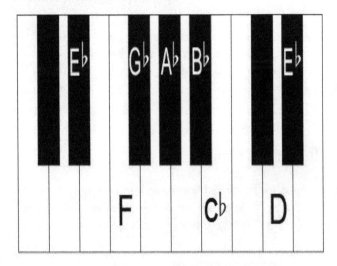

Here's the E flat harmonic minor scale on the treble clef.

E flat harmonic minor scale

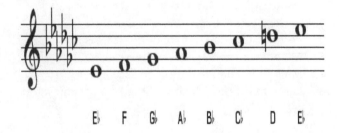

Here's the E flat harmonic minor scale on the bass clef.

E flat harmonic minor scale

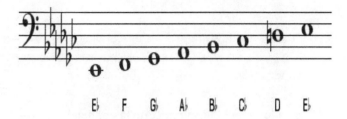

E Flat Melodic Minor Scale

Let's now learn how to form the E flat melodic minor scale. While the harmonic minor scale raises only the seventh note of the natural minor scale by a half step, the melodic minor scale raises both the sixth and seventh notes by a half step.

The notes of the E flat natural minor scale (as we've seen) are E ♭ , F, G ♭ , A ♭ , B ♭ , C ♭ , D ♭ , E ♭ . For the E flat melodic minor scale we raise the 6th and 7th notes by a half step and this results in E ♭ , F, G ♭ , A ♭ , B ♭ , C, D, E ♭ . These notes are used when ascending. When descending, you go back to the natural minor scale.

Notes of the Eb melodic minor scale ascending: E ♭ , F, G ♭ , A ♭ , B ♭ , C, D, E ♭ .

Notes of the Eb melodic minor scale descending: E ♭ , F, G ♭ , A ♭ , B ♭ , C ♭ , D ♭ , E ♭ . (These are the notes of the Eb natural minor scale.)

The formula for a melodic minor scale (ascending) is W-H-W-W-W-W-H. The descending formula is the natural minor scale formula backwards.

Melodic E flat Minor Scale Intervals

1. Tonic: The 1st note of the Eb melodic minor scale is Eb.
2. Major 2nd: The 2nd note of the scale is F.
3. Minor 3rd: The 3rd note of the scale is Gb.
4. Perfect 4th: The 4th note of the scale is Ab.
5. Perfect 5th: The 5th note is Bb.
6. Major 6th: The 6th note is C.
7. Major 7th: The 7th note is D.
8. Perfect 8th: The 8th note of the Eb melodic minor scale is Eb.

Here's the E-flat melodic minor scale on piano, ascending.

E flat melodic minor scale (ascending)

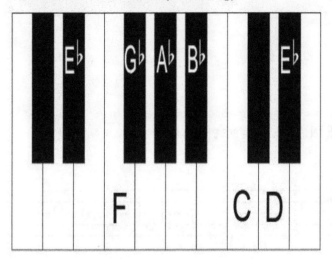

Here's the E flat melodic minor scale on the treble clef.

E flat melodic minor scale (ascending)

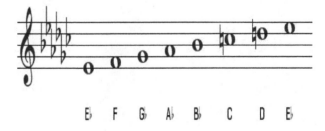

Here's the scale on the bass clef.

E flat melodic minor scale (ascending)

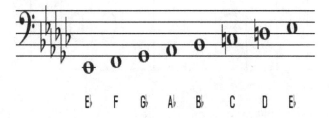

E♭ F G♭ A♭ B♭ C D E♭

The E Minor Scale – Natural, Harmonic and Melodic

This lesson is all about the E minor scale. There are three types of minor scales and we shall take a look at all of them here. They are the natural, melodic and harmonic minor scales.

E Natural Minor Scale

Let's start with the E natural minor scale. This scale consists of the pitches, E, F♯, G, A, B, C, and D. Its key signature consists of one sharp.

Highly Recommended: Click here for one of the BEST piano/keyboard courses I've seen online.

Em Scale Note Intervals

1. Tonic: E is the 1st note of the E natural minor scale.
2. Major 2nd: F# is the 2nd note of the scale.
3. Minor 3rd: G is the 3rd note of the scale.
4. Perfect 4th: A is the 4th note of the scale.
5. Perfect 5th: B is the 5th note of the scale.
6. Minor 6th: C is the 6th note of the scale.
7. Minor 7th: D is the 7th note of the scale.

8. **Perfect 8th:** E (one octave higher) is the 8th note of the D natural minor scale.

Here's the E minor scale on the treble clef.

E minor scale (treble clef)

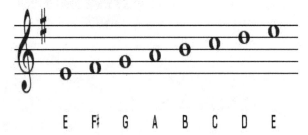

E F# G A B C D E

Here's the Em scale on the bass clef.

E minor scale (bass clef)

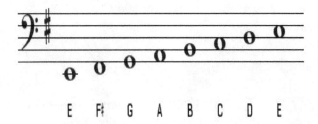

E F# G A B C D E

Here's the Em scale on the piano keyboard.

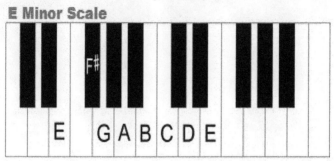

E Minor Scale

Scale Degrees:

1. Tonic: E
2. Supertonic: F#
3. Mediant: G
4. Subdominant: A
5. Dominant: B
6. Submediant: C
7. Subtonic: D
8. Octave: E

The relative major key for the key of E minor is G major. A natural minor scale/key consists of the same notes as its relative major. The notes of the G major scale are G, A, B, C, D, E, F#. As we've seen, the E natural minor uses these same notes, except that the sixth note of the major scale becomes the root note of its relative minor.

The formula for forming a natural (or pure) minor scale is W-H-W-W-H-W-W. "W" stands for whole step and "H" stands for half step. To build an E natural minor scale, starting on E, we take a whole step to F#. Next, we take a half step to G. From G, a whole step takes us to A. Another whole step takes us to B. From B, we go up a half step to C. From C, we take a whole step to D. Lastly, one more whole step returns us to E, one octave higher.

What are the fingerings for the E minor scale? They are as follows:

- Notes: E, F#, G, A, B, C, D, E
- Fingerings (Left Hand): 5, 4, 3, 2, 1, 3, 2, 1
- Fingerings (Right Hand): 1, 2, 3, 1, 2, 3, 4, 5

Thumb: 1, index finger: 2, middle finger: 3, ring finger: 4 and pinky finger: 5.

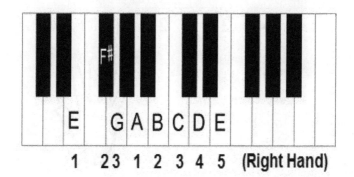

E   G A B   C D E

1   2 3   1   2   3   4   5   (Right Hand)

E Minor Scale
Right Hand
Fingering

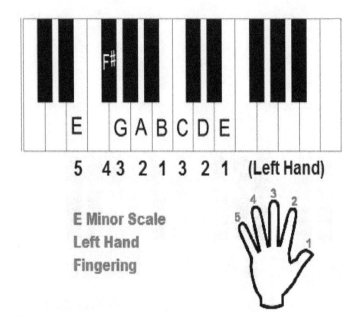

**E Minor Scale
Left Hand
Fingering**

Video – How to play Em scale on piano/keyboard:

Let's now take a look at the chords in the key of E minor.

1. Chord i: E minor. Its notes are E – G – B.
2. Chord ii: F# diminished. Its notes are F# – A – C.
3. Chord III: G major. Its notes are G – B – D.
4. Chord iv: A minor. Its notes are A – C – E.
5. Chord v: B minor. Its notes are B – D – F#.
6. Chord VI: C major. Its notes are C – E – G.
7. Chord VII: D major. Its notes are D – F# – A.

What are the chords in the key of E minor natural? All about the key of Em and its chords.

Video – Chords in the Key of Em:

E Harmonic Minor Scale

Let's now take a look at the E harmonic minor scale.

To play a harmonic minor scale, you simply raise the seventh note of the natural minor scale by a half-step as you go up and down the scale. For example:

Natural E Minor Scale = E, F♯, G, A, B, C, D, E

Harmonic E Minor Scale = E, F♯, G, A, B, C, D#, E

The formula for forming a harmonic minor scale is W-H-W-W-H-W 1/2-H. (Whole step – half step – whole step – whole step – half step – whole step and a 1/2 step – half step.)

Harmonic Em Scale Intervals

1. Tonic: The 1st note of the E harmonic minor scale is E.
2. Major 2nd: The 2nd note of the scale is F#.
3. Minor 3rd: The 3rd note of the scale is G.
4. Perfect 4th: The 4th note of the scale is A.
5. Perfect 5th: The 5th is B.
6. Minor 6th: The 6th note is C.
7. Major 7th: The 7th note is D#.

8. Perfect 8th: The 8th note is E.

Here's a diagram of the harmonic E minor scale on piano.

E harmonic minor scale

Here's the scale on the treble clef.

E harmonic minor scale

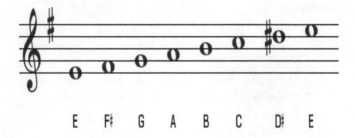

Here's the scale on the bass clef.

E harmonic minor scale

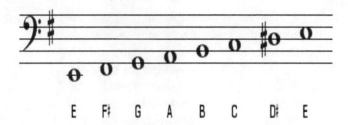

E F# G A B C D# E

E Melodic Minor Scale

For the melodic minor scale, you raise the sixth and seventh notes of a scale by a half step as you go up the scale and then return to the natural minor as you go down the scale. The notes of the E melodic minor scale ascending are: E, F♯, G, A, B, C#, D#, E. The notes of the A melodic minor scale descending are:E, F♯, G, A, B, C, D, E (E natural minor scale).

The formula for a melodic minor scale is whole step – half step – whole step – whole step – whole step – whole step – half step. (W-H-W-W-W-W-H) The descending formula is the natural minor scale formula backwards.

Melodic Em Scale Intervals

1. Tonic: The 1st note of the E melodic minor scale is E.

2. Major 2nd: The 2nd note of the scale is F#.
3. Minor 3rd: The 3rd note of the scale is G.
4. Perfect 4th: The 4th note of the scale is A.
5. Perfect 5th: The 5th note of the scale is B.
6. Major 6th: The 6th note of the scale is C#.
7. Major 7th: The 7th note of the scale is D#.
8. Perfect 8th: The 8th note of the scale is E.

Here's a diagram of the melodic E minor scale on piano.

E melodic minor scale (ascending)

Here's the scale on the treble clef.

E melodic minor scale

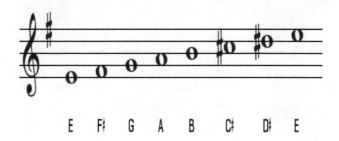

E F♯ G A B C♯ D♯ E

Here's the scale on the bass clef.

E melodic minor scale

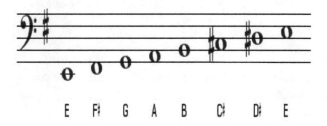

E F♯ G A B C♯ D♯ E

Remember that for the melodic minor scale, when descending, you play the natural minor scale.

F Minor Scale – Notes, Chords and More

This lesson is all about the F minor scale. We will take a look at the three types of minor scale, the natural minor, melodic minor and harmonic minor scales.

F Natural Minor Scale

Let's start with the F natural minor scale. This scale consists of the pitches, F, G, A ♭ , B ♭ , C, D ♭ , and E ♭ . It has four flats.

To learn more about this scale and others, check out my course, **Learn Scales & Music Theory & Give Yourself An Upper Hand.**

Fm Scale Note Intervals

1. Tonic: F is the 1st note of the F natural minor scale.
2. Major 2nd: G is the 2nd note of the scale.
3. Minor 3rd: Ab is the 3rd note of the scale.
4. Perfect 4th: Bb is the 4th note of the scale.
5. Perfect 5th: C is the 5th note of the scale.
6. Minor 6th: Db is the 6th note of the scale.
7. Minor 7th: Eb is the 7th note of the scale.

8. **Perfect 8th:** F (one octave higher) is the 8th note of the B natural minor scale.

Here's a diagram of the F natural minor scale on the treble clef.

F minor scale (treble clef)

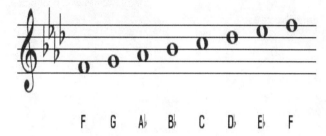

F   G   A♭   B♭   C   D♭   E♭   F

Here's the F natural minor scale on the bass clef.

F minor scale (bass clef)

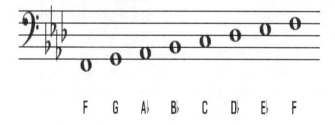

F   G   A♭   B♭   C   D♭   E♭   F

Here's the F natural minor scale on piano.

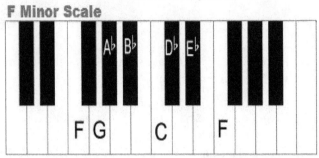

F Minor Scale

Fm Scale Degrees:

1. Tonic: F
2. Supertonic: G
3. Mediant: Ab
4. Subdominant: Bb
5. Dominant: C
6. Submediant: Db
7. Subtonic: Eb
8. Octave: F

The relative major of F minor is Ab major. Minor keys and their relative major make use of the same notes. The notes of the F minor scale as we've seen are F, G, A ♭ , B ♭ , C, D ♭ , and E ♭ . For the Ab major scale, it's A ♭ , B ♭ , C, D ♭ , E ♭ , F and G. The difference is the root note of the two scales. The sixth note of a major scale becomes the root note of its relative minor.

You can memorize this formula to form any natural minor scale: whole step – half step – whole step – whole step – half step – whole step – whole step or w – h – w – w – h – w – w. (A whole step skips a key while a half step moves to the next key.) Let's try this with the F minor scale. Let's start on F and move a whole step to G. From G move a half step to Ab. Next, we move a whole step from Ab to Bb. From Bb, let's move a whole step to C. Next, we go up a half step from C to Db. From Db, we move up one whole step to Eb. Finally, we move a whole step from Eb to F.

What are the fingerings for the F minor scale? They are as follows:

- Notes: F, G, Ab, Bb, C, Db, Eb, F
- Fingerings (Left Hand): 5, 4, 3, 2, 1, 3, 2, 1
- Fingerings (Right Hand): 1, 2, 3, 4, 1, 2, 3, 4

Thumb: 1, index finger: 2, middle finger: 3, ring finger: 4 and pinky finger: 5.

Let's now take a look at the chords in the key of F minor.

1. Chord i: F minor. Its notes are F – Ab – C.
2. Chord ii: G diminished. Its notes are G – Bb – Db.
3. Chord III: Ab major. Its notes are Ab – C – Eb.
4. Chord iv: Bb minor. Its notes are Bb – Db – F.
5. Chord v: C minor. Its notes are C – Eb – G.
6. Chord VI: Db major. Its notes are Db – F – Ab.
7. Chord VII: Eb major. Its notes are Eb – G – Bb.

F Harmonic Minor Scale

Let's now take a look at the F harmonic minor scale.

The harmonic minor scale raises the seventh note of the natural minor scale by a half-step, when ascending and descending the scale. For example, the notes of the F natural minor scale are F – G – A ♭ - B ♭ - C – D ♭ - E ♭ - F. For the F harmonic minor scale, the notes are F – G – A ♭ - B ♭ - C – D ♭ - E – F. The seventh note of the scale has been changed from Eb to E. It's now a half step (or semitone) higher.

The formula for forming a harmonic minor scale is W-H-W-W-H-W 1/2-H.

Harmonic Minor Scale Intervals

1. Tonic: The 1st note of the F harmonic minor scale is F.
2. Major 2nd: The 2nd note of the scale is G.
3. Minor 3rd: The 3rd note of the scale is Ab.
4. Perfect 4th: The 4th note of the scale is Bb.
5. Perfect 5th: The 5th note of the scale is C.
6. Minor 6th: The 6th note of the scale is Db.
7. Major 7th: The 7th note of the scale is Eb.
8. Perfect 8th: The 8th note of the scale is F.

Here's a diagram of the F harmonic minor scale on piano.

F harmonic minor scale

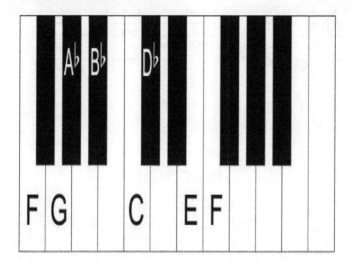

Here's the F harmonic minor scale on the treble clef.

F harmonic minor scale

F   G   A♭   B♭   C   D♭   E   F

Here's the F harmonic minor scale on the bass clef.

F harmonic minor scale

F   G   A♭   B♭   C   D♭   E   F

F Melodic Minor Scale

Let's now take a look at the melodic minor scale. For this scale, you raise the sixth and seventh notes by a half step as you go up the scale and then return to the natural minor as you go down the scale. The notes of the F melodic minor scale ascending are: F – G – A♭ - B♭ - C – D – E – F. The notes of the B melodic minor scale descending are: F – G – A♭ - B♭ - C – D♭ - E♭ - F.

The formula for a melodic minor scale is W-H-W-W-W-W-H. The descending formula is the natural minor scale formula backwards.

Melodic F Minor Scale Intervals

1. Tonic: The 1st note of the F melodic minor scale is F.
2. Major 2nd: The 2nd note of the scale is G.

3. Minor 3rd: The 3rd is Ab.
4. Perfect 4th: The 4th note is Bb.
5. Perfect 5th: The 5th note is C.
6. Major 6th: The 6th is D.
7. Major 7th: The 7th is E.
8. Perfect 8th: The 8th note of the scale is F.

Here's a diagram of the melodic F minor scale on piano.

F melodic minor scale

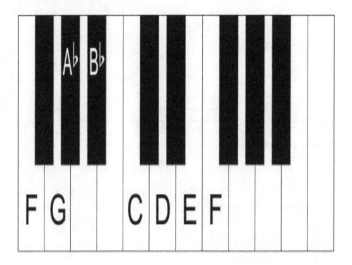

Here's the scale on the treble clef.

F melodic minor scale

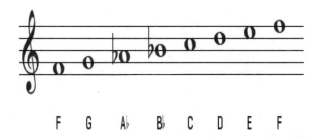

F   G   A♭   B♭   C   D   E   F

Here's the scale on the bass clef.

F melodic minor scale

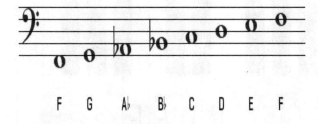

F   G   A♭   B♭   C   D   E   F

Remember that for the melodic minor scale, when descending, you play the natural minor scale

The G Minor Scale (Gm)

This lesson is all about the G minor scale. We will take a look at the three types of minor scale, the natural minor, melodic minor and harmonic minor scales.

G Natural Minor Scale

Let's start with the G natural minor scale. This scale consists of the pitches, G, A, B ♭ , C, D, E ♭ , and F. It has two flats.

Highly Recommended: Click here for one of the BEST piano/keyboard courses I've seen online.

Gm Scale Note Intervals:

1. Tonic: G is the 1st note of the G natural minor scale.
2. Major 2nd: A is the 2nd note of the scale.
3. Minor 3rd: Bb is the 3rd note of the scale.
4. Perfect 4th: C is the 4th note of the scale.
5. Perfect 5th: D is the 5th note of the scale.
6. Minor 6th: Eb is the 6th note of the scale.
7. Minor 7th: F is the 7th note of the scale.
8. Perfect 8th: G (one octave higher) is the 8th note of the B natural minor scale.

Here's a diagram of the G natural minor scale on the treble

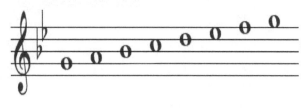

clef.

Here's the G minor scale on the bass clef.

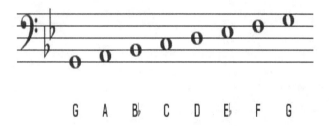

Here's the G minor scale on piano.

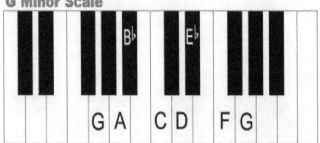

Gm Scale Degrees:

1. Tonic: G
2. Supertonic: A
3. Mediant: Bb
4. Subdominant: C
5. Dominant: D
6. Submediant: Eb
7. Subtonic: F
8. Octave: G

The relative major of G minor is Bb major. Minor keys and their relative major make use of the same notes. The notes of the G minor scale as we've seen are G, A, B♭, C, D, E♭, and F. For the Bb major scale, it's B♭, C, D, E♭, F, G and A. The difference is the root note of the two scales. The sixth note of a major scale becomes the root note of its relative minor.

You can memorize this formula to form any natural minor scale: whole step – half step – whole step – whole step – half step – whole step – whole step or w – h – w – w – h – w – w. (A whole step skips a key while a half step moves to the next key.) Let's try this with the G minor scale. Let's start on G and move a whole step to A. From A move a half step to Bb. Next, we move a whole step from Bb to C. From C, let's move a whole step to D. Next, we go up a half step from D to Eb. From Eb, we move up one whole step to F. Finally, we move a whole step from F to G.

What are the fingerings for the G minor scale? They are as follows:

- Notes: G, A, Bb, C, D, Eb, F, G

- Fingerings (Left Hand): 5, 4, 3, 2, 1, 3, 2, 1
- Fingerings (Right Hand): 1, 2, 3, 1, 2, 3, 4, 5

Thumb: 1, index finger: 2, middle finger: 3, ring finger: 4 and pinky finger: 5.

Let's now take a look at the chords in the key of G minor.

1. Chord i: G minor. Its notes are G – Bb – D.
2. Chord ii: A diminished. Its notes are A – C – Eb.
3. Chord III: Bb major. Its notes are Bb – D – F.
4. Chord iv: C minor. Its notes are C – Eb – G.
5. Chord v: D minor. Its notes are D – F – A.
6. Chord VI: Eb major. Its notes are Eb – G – Bb.
7. Chord VII: F major. Its notes are F – A – C.

G Harmonic Minor Scale

Let's now take a look at the G harmonic minor scale.

The harmonic minor scale raises the seventh note of the natural minor scale by a half-step, when ascending and descending the scale. For example, the notes of the G natural minor scale are G – A – B ♭ - C – D – E ♭ - F – G. For the G harmonic minor scale, the notes are G – A – B ♭ - C – D – E ♭ - F# – G. The seventh note of the scale has been changed from F to F#. It's now a half step (or semitone) higher.

The formula for forming a harmonic minor scale is W-H-W-W-H-W 1/2-H.

Harmonic Minor Scale Intervals

1. Tonic: The 1st note of the G harmonic minor scale is G.
2. Major 2nd: The 2nd note of the scale is A.
3. Minor 3rd: The 3rd note of the scale is Bb.
4. Perfect 4th: The 4th note of the scale is C.
5. Perfect 5th: The 5th note of the scale is D.
6. Minor 6th: The 6th note of the scale is Eb.
7. Major 7th: The 7th note of the scale is F#.
8. Perfect 8th: The 8th note of the scale is G.

Here's a diagram of the G harmonic minor scale on piano.

G harmonic minor scale

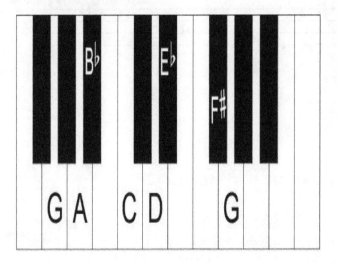

Here's the G harmonic minor scale on the treble clef.

G harmonic minor scale

G A B♭ C D E♭ F♯ G

Here's the G harmonic minor scale on the bass clef.

G harmonic minor scale

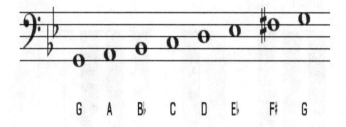

G A B♭ C D E♭ F♯ G

G Melodic Minor Scale

Let's now take a look at the melodic minor scale. For this scale, you raise the sixth and seventh notes by a half step as you go up the scale and then return to the natural minor as you go down the scale. The notes of the G melodic minor scale ascending are: G – A – B♭ - C – D – E – F# – G. The notes of the G melodic minor scale descending are: G, A, B♭, C, D, E♭, and F.

The formula for a melodic minor scale is W-H-W-W-W-W-H. The descending formula is the natural minor scale formula backwards.

Melodic G Minor Scale Intervals

1. Tonic: The 1st note of the G melodic minor scale is G.
2. Major 2nd: The 2nd note of the scale is A.
3. Minor 3rd: The 3rd is Bb.
4. Perfect 4th: The 4th note is C.
5. Perfect 5th: The 5th note is D.
6. Major 6th: The 6th is E.
7. Major 7th: The 7th is F#.
8. Perfect 8th: The 8th note of the scale is G.

Here's a diagram of the melodic G minor scale on piano.

G melodic minor scale (ascending)

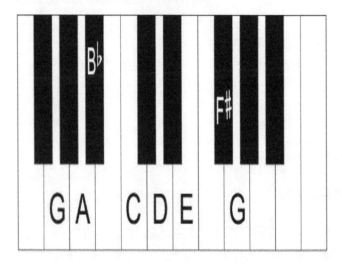

Here's the scale on the treble clef.

G melodic minor scale

Here's the scale on the bass clef.

G melodic minor scale

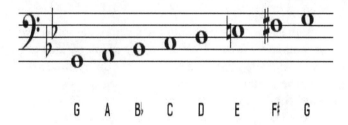

G A B♭ C D E F♯ G

Remember that for the melodic minor scale, when descending, you play the natural minor scale.

A Flat Minor Scale

In this lesson, we will learn how to play the A flat minor scale. The three types of minor scales are the natural, melodic and harmonic minor scales. We will take a look at all three of them here.

We will learn the notes, intervals and scale degrees of the A flat minor scale (natural, melodic and harmonic) on the piano, treble and bass clef.

A flat is an enharmonic of G sharp. On piano, the same keys are used to play the two scales. In terms of sound, they are identical. The only difference is the names of the notes. The notes of the G sharp natural minor scale are G#, A#, B, C#, D#, E, F#, G#.

The A Flat Natural Minor Scale

The notes of the A flat natural minor scale are Ab, Bb, Cb, Db, Eb, Fb and Gb. This scale has 7 flats.

Let's take a look at the intervals of the Ab minor scale.

1. *Tonic – The 1st note of the A-flat natural minor scale is Ab.*
2. *Major 2nd – The 2nd note of the scale is Bb.*
3. *Minor 3rd – The 3rd note of the scale is Cb.*
4. *Perfect 4th – The 4th note of the scale is Db.*

5. *Perfect 5th – The 5th note of the scale is Eb.*
6. *Minor 6th – The 6th note of the scale is Fb.*
7. *Minor 7th – The 7th note of the scale is Gb.*
8. *Perfect 8th – The 8th note of the A-flat natural minor scale is Ab.*

Here's a diagram of the A flat minor scale on piano/keyboard.

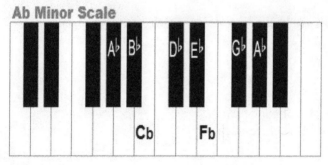

Here's the A flat natural minor scale on the treble clef.

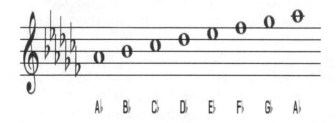

Here's the A flat natural minor scale on the bass clef.

A flat minor scale

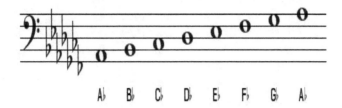

How about the scale degrees? They are as follows:

1. *Tonic: Ab*
2. *Supertonic: Bb*
3. *Mediant: Cb*
4. *Subdominant: Db*
5. *Dominant: Eb*
6. *Submediant: Fb*
7. *Subtonic: Gb*
8. *Octave: Ab*

There's a formula for forming natural minor scales using whole steps and half steps. That formula is W-H-W-W-H-W-W. "W" stands for whole step and "H" stands for half step.

Let's form the A flat minor scale with this formula. Of course, our starting note is Ab. From Ab, we take a whole step to Bb. Next, we take a half step to Cb. From Cb, a whole step takes us to Db. Another whole step takes us to Eb. From Eb, we go up a half step to Fb. From Fb, a whole step takes us to Gb. Finally, the last whole step returns us to Ab.

The relative major key for the key of Ab minor is Cb major. A natural minor scale/key consists of the same notes as its relative major. The sixth note of the major scale becomes the root note of its relative minor.

Let's now learn the piano fingerings for the A flat minor scale.

On both the left and right hands, the thumb is finger 1, index finger is finger two, middle finger is finger 3, ring finger is finger 4 and pinky (little) finger is finger 5.

- *G Sharp Minor Notes: G#, A#, B, C#, D#, E, F#, G#*
- *A Flat Minor Notes: Ab, Bb, Cb, Db, Eb, Fb, Gb, Ab*
- *Fingerings (Left Hand): 3, 2, 1, 3, 2, 1, 3, 2*
- *Fingerings (Right Hand): 2, 3, 1, 2, 3, 1, 2, 3*

Triad chords in the key of Ab minor and their notes:

1. *Chord i – A flat minor. Notes: Ab – Cb – Eb*
2. *Chord iidim – B flat diminished. Notes: Bb – Db – Fb*
3. *Chord III – C flat major. Notes: Cb – Eb – Gb*
4. *Chord iv – D flat minor. Notes: Db – Fb – Ab*
5. *Chord v – E flat minor. Notes: Eb – Gb – Bb*
6. *Chord VI – F flat major. Notes: Fb – Ab – Cb*
7. *Chord VII – G flat major. Notes: Gb – Bb – Db*

A Flat Harmonic Minor Scale

Now that we know the notes of the A flat minor scale (natural), we now take a look at the A flat harmonic minor scale.

To play a harmonic minor scale, you simply raise the seventh note of the natural minor scale by a half-step as you go up and down the scale. For example, the notes of the natural A flat minor scale are Ab, Bb, Cb, Db, Eb, Fb, Gb and Ab. To form the A flat harmonic minor scale, we raise the seventh note by a half step and this results in Ab, Bb, Cb, Db, Eb, Fb, G and Ab.

The formula for forming a harmonic minor scale is W-H-W-W-H-W 1/2-H. (Whole step – half step – whole step – whole step – half step – whole step and a 1/2 step – half step.)

Harmonic Minor Scale Intervals

1. Tonic: The 1st note of the Ab harmonic minor scale is Ab.
2. Major 2nd: The 2nd note of the scale is Bb.
3. Minor 3rd: The 3rd note of the scale is Cb.
4. Perfect 4th: The 4th note of the scale is Db.
5. Perfect 5th: The 5th note of the scale is Eb.
6. Minor 6th: The 6th note of the scale is Fb.
7. Major 7th: The 7th note of the scale is G.
8. Perfect 8th: The 8th note of the Ab harmonic minor scale is Ab.

Here's a diagram of the harmonic A flat minor scale on piano.

A flat harmonic minor scale

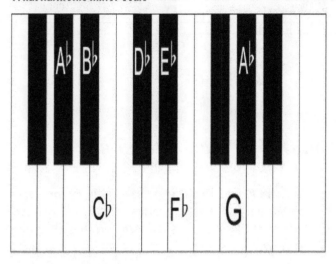

Here's the A flat harmonic minor scale on the treble clef.

A flat harmonic minor scale

Here's the A flat harmonic minor scale on the bass clef.

A flat harmonic minor scale

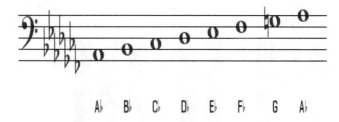

Ab　Bb　Cb　Db　Eb　Fb　G　Ab

A Flat Melodic Minor Scale

Let's now learn how to form the A flat melodic minor scale. While the harmonic minor scale raises only the seventh note of the natural minor scale by a half step, the melodic minor scale raises both the sixth and seventh notes by a half step.

The notes of the A flat natural minor scale (as we've seen) are Ab – Bb – Cb – Db – Eb – Fb – Gb – Ab. For the A flat melodic minor scale we raise the 6th and 7th notes by a half step and this results in Ab – Bb – Cb – Db – Eb – F – G – Ab. These notes are used when ascending. When descending, you go back to the natural minor scale.

Notes of the Ab melodic minor scale ascending: Ab, Bb, Cb, Db, Eb, F, G, Ab.

Notes of the Ab melodic minor scale descending: Ab, Bb, Cb, Db, Eb, Fb, Gb, Ab. (These are the notes of the Ab natural minor scale.)

The formula for a melodic minor scale (ascending) is W-H-W-W-W-W-H. The descending formula is the natural minor scale formula backwards.

Melodic A flat Minor Scale Intervals

1. *Tonic: The 1st note of the Ab melodic minor scale is Ab.*
2. *Major 2nd: The 2nd note of the scale is Bb.*
3. *Minor 3rd: The 3rd note of the scale is Cb.*
4. *Perfect 4th: The 4th note of the scale is Db.*
5. *Perfect 5th: The 5th note is Eb.*
6. *Major 6th: The 6th note is Fb.*
7. *Major 7th: The 7th note is Gb.*
8. *Perfect 8th: The 8th note of the Ab melodic minor scale is Ab.*

Here's the A-flat melodic minor scale on piano, ascending.

A flat melodic minor scale (ascending)

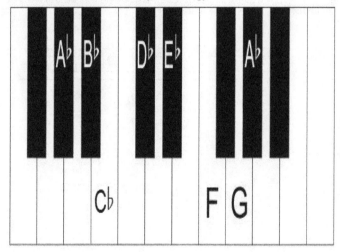

Here's the A flat melodic minor scale on the treble clef.

A flat melodic minor scale (ascending)

Ab Bb Cb Db Eb F G Ab

Here's the scale on the bass clef.

A flat melodic minor scale (ascending)

Ab Bb Cb Db Eb F G Ab

The A Minor Scale

This lesson is all about the A minor scale. There are three types of minor scales and we shall take a look at all of them here. They are the natural, melodic and harmonic minor scales.

A Natural Minor Scale

Let's start with the A natural minor scale. This scale consists of the pitches, A, B, C, D, E, F and G. It has no sharp or flat notes.

Note Intervals

1. Tonic: A is the 1st note of the A natural minor scale.
2. Major 2nd: B is the 2nd note of the scale.
3. Minor 3rd: C is the 3rd note of the scale.
4. Perfect 4th: D is the 4th note of the scale.
5. Perfect 5th: E is the 5th note of the scale.
6. Minor 6th: F is the 6th note of the scale.
7. Minor 7th: G is the 7th note of the scale.
8. Perfect 8th: A (one octave higher) is the 8th note of the A natural minor scale.

My #1 Recommendation: Go here to learn about the BEST piano/keyboard course I've seen online.

Here's the A minor scale on the treble clef.

A Minor Scale (Treble Clef)

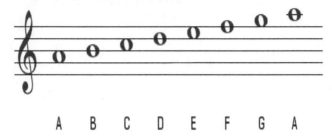

Here's the A minor scale on the bass clef.

A Minor Scale (Bass Clef)

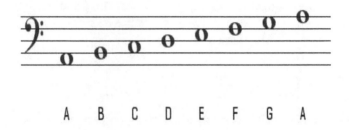

Here's the Am scale on piano.

A Minor Scale

Scale Degrees of Am Scale:

1. Tonic: A
2. Supertonic: B
3. Mediant: C
4. Subdominant: D
5. Dominant: E
6. Submediant: F
7. Subtonic: G
8. Octave: A

The relative major key for the key of A minor is C major. A natural minor scale/key consists of the same notes as its relative major. The notes of the C major scale are C, D, E, F, G, A and B. As we've seen, the A natural minor uses these same notes, except that the sixth note of the major scale becomes the root note of its relative minor.

The formula for forming a natural (or pure) minor scale is W-H-W-W-H-W-W. "W" stands for whole step and "H" stands for half step. To build an A natural minor scale, starting on A, we take a whole step to B. Next, we take a half step to C. From C, a whole step takes us to D. Another whole step takes us to E. From E, we go up a half step to F. From F, we take a whole step to G. Lastly, one more whole step returns us to A, one octave higher.

What are the fingerings for the A minor scale? They are as follows:

- Notes: A, B, C, D, E, F, G, A
- Fingerings (Left Hand): 5, 4, 3, 2, 1, 3, 2, 1
- Fingerings (Right Hand): 1, 2, 3, 1, 2, 3, 4, 5

Thumb: 1, index finger: 2, middle finger: 3, ring finger: 4 and pinky finger: 5.

Video: How to Play the A Minor Scale

Chords In The Key of A Minor

Let's now take a look at the chords in the key of A minor.

1. Chord i: A minor. Its notes are A – C – E.
2. Chord ii: B diminished. Its notes are B – D – F.
3. Chord III: C major. Its notes are C – E – G.
4. Chord iv: D minor. Its notes are D – F – A.
5. Chord v: E minor. Its notes are E – G – B.
6. Chord VI: F major. Its notes are F – A – C.
7. Chord VII: G major. Its notes are G – B – D.

A Harmonic Minor Scale

Let's now take a look at the A harmonic minor scale.

To play a harmonic minor scale, you simply raise the seventh note of the natural minor scale by a half-step as you go up and down the scale. For example:

Natural A Minor Scale = A – B – C – D – E – F – G – A

Harmonic A Minor Scale = A – B – C – D – E – F – G# – A

The formula for forming a harmonic minor scale is W-H-W-W-H-W 1/2-H. (Whole step – half step – whole step – whole step – half step – whole step and a 1/2 step – half step.)

Harmonic Minor Scale Intervals

1. Tonic: The 1st note of the A harmonic minor scale is A.
2. Major 2nd: The 2nd note of the scale is B.
3. Minor 3rd: The 3rd note of the scale is C.
4. Perfect 4th: The 4th note of the scale is D.
5. Perfect 5th: The 5th is E.
6. Minor 6th: The 6th note is F.
7. Major 7th: The 7th note is G#.
8. Perfect 8th: The 8th note is A.

Here's a diagram of the A harmonic minor scale on piano.

Harmonic Minor Scale

Here's the A minor scale (harmonic) on the treble clef.

A harmonic minor scale

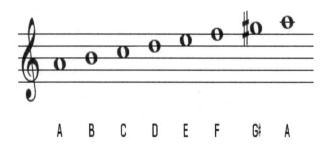

A   B   C   D   E   F   G#   A

Here's the A minor scale (harmonic) on the bass clef.

A harmonic minor scale

A   B   C   D   E   F   G#   A

A Melodic Minor Scale

For the melodic minor scale, you raise the sixth and seventh notes of the natural minor scale by a half step as you go up the scale and then return to the natural minor as you go down the scale. The notes of the A melodic minor scale ascending are: A – B – C – D – E – F# – G# – A. The notes of the A melodic minor scale descending are: A – B – C – D – E – F – G – A (A natural minor scale).

The formula for a melodic minor scale is whole step – half step – whole step – whole step – whole step – whole step – half step. (W-H-W-W-W-W-H). The descending formula is the natural minor scale formula backwards.

A Melodic Minor Scale Intervals:

1. Tonic: The 1st note of the A melodic minor scale is A.
2. Major 2nd: The 2nd note of the scale is B.
3. Minor 3rd: The 3rd note of the scale is C.
4. Perfect 4th: The 4th note of the scale is D.
5. Perfect 5th: The 5th note of the scale is E.
6. Major 6th: The 6th note of the scale is F#.
7. Major 7th: The 7th note of the scale is G#.
8. Perfect 8th: The 8th note of the scale is A.

Here's a diagram of the A melodic minor scale on piano (ascending).

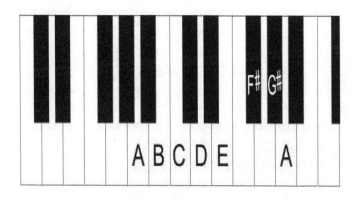

A melodic minor scale (ascending)

Here's the scale on the treble clef (ascending).

Here's the scale on the bass clef (ascending).

A melodic minor scale

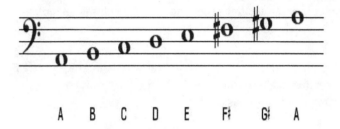

A   B   C   D   E   F♯   G♯   A

Remember that for the melodic minor scale, when descending, you play the natural minor scale.

B Flat Minor Scale

In this lesson, we will learn how to play the B flat minor scale. The three types of minor scales are the natural, melodic and harmonic minor scales. We will take a look at all three of them here.

We will learn the notes, intervals and scale degrees of the B flat minor scale (natural, melodic and harmonic) on the piano, treble and bass clef.

B flat is an enharmonic of A sharp. On piano, the same keys are used to play the two scales. In terms of sound, they are identical. The only difference is the names of the notes. The notes of the A sharp natural minor scale are A♯, B♯, C♯, D♯, E♯, F♯, and G♯.

B Flat Natural Minor Scale

The notes of the B flat natural minor scale are B♭, C, D♭, E♭, F, G♭, and A♭. This scale has 5 flats.

Let's take a look at the intervals of the Bb minor scale.

Note Intervals:

1. Tonic – The 1st note of the B-flat natural minor scale is Bb.
2. Major 2nd – The 2nd note of the scale is C.
3. Minor 3rd – The 3rd note of the scale is Db.
4. Perfect 4th – The 4th note of the scale is Eb.
5. Perfect 5th – The 5th note of the scale is F.
6. Minor 6th – The 6th note of the scale is Gb.
7. Minor 7th – The 7th note of the scale is Ab.
8. Perfect 8th – The 8th note of the A-flat natural minor scale is Bb.

Here's a diagram of the B flat minor scale on piano/keyboard.

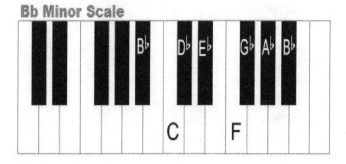

Here's the B flat natural minor scale on the treble clef.

Here's the B flat natural minor scale on the bass clef.

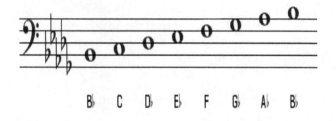

How about the scale degrees? They are as follows:

1. Tonic: Bb
2. Supertonic: C
3. Mediant: Db
4. Subdominant: Eb
5. Dominant: F
6. Submediant: Gb
7. Subtonic: Ab
8. Octave: Bb

There's a formula for forming natural minor scales using whole steps and half steps. That formula is W-H-W-W-H-W-W. "W" stands for whole step and "H" stands for half step.

Let's form the B flat minor scale with this formula. Of course, our starting note is Bb. From Bb, we take a whole step to C. Next, we take a half step to Db. From Db, a whole step takes us to Eb. Another whole step takes us to F. From F, we go up a half step to Gb. From Gb, a whole step takes us to Ab. Finally, the last whole step returns us to Bb.

The relative major key for the key of Bb minor is Db major. A natural minor scale/key consists of the same notes as its relative major. The sixth note of the major scale becomes the root note of its relative minor.

Let's now learn the piano fingerings for the Bb minor scale.

On both the left and right hands, the thumb is finger 1, index finger is finger two, middle finger is finger 3, ring finger is finger 4 and pinky (little) finger is finger 5.

- A Sharp Minor Notes: A♯, B♯, C♯, D♯, E♯, F♯, G♯, A♯
- B Flat Minor Notes: B♭, C, D♭, E♭, F, G♭, A♭, B♭
- Fingerings (Left Hand): 2, 1, 3, 2, 1, 4, 3, 2
- Fingerings (Right Hand): 2, 1, 2, 3, 1, 2, 3, 4

Triad chords in the key of Bb minor and their notes:

1. Chord i – B flat minor. Notes: Bb – Db – F
2. Chord iidim – C diminished. Notes: C – Eb- Gb

3. Chord III – D flat major. Notes: Db – F – Ab
4. Chord iv – E flat minor. Notes: Eb – Gb – Bb
5. Chord v – F minor. Notes: F – Ab – C
6. Chord VI – G flat major. Notes: Gb – Bb – Db
7. Chord VII – A flat major. Notes: Ab – C – Eb

B Flat Harmonic Minor Scale

Now that we know the notes of the B flat minor scale (natural), we now take a look at the B flat harmonic minor scale.

To play a harmonic minor scale, you simply raise the seventh note of the natural minor scale by a half-step as you go up and down the scale. For example, the notes of the natural B flat minor scale are B ♭ , C, D ♭ , E ♭ , F, G ♭ , A ♭ , B ♭ . To form the B flat harmonic minor scale, we raise the seventh note by a half step and this results in B ♭ , C, D ♭ , E ♭ , F, G ♭ , A, B ♭ .

The formula for forming a harmonic minor scale is W-H-W-W-H-W 1/2-H. (Whole step – half step – whole step – whole step – half step – whole step and a 1/2 step – half step.)

Harmonic Minor Scale Intervals

1. Tonic: The 1st note of the Bb harmonic minor scale is Bb.
2. Major 2nd: The 2nd note of the scale is C.
3. Minor 3rd: The 3rd note of the scale is Db.
4. Perfect 4th: The 4th note of the scale is Eb.
5. Perfect 5th: The 5th note of the scale is F.
6. Minor 6th: The 6th note of the scale is Gb.
7. Major 7th: The 7th note of the scale is A.
8. Perfect 8th: The 8th note of the Bb harmonic minor scale is Bb.

Here's a diagram of the harmonic B flat minor scale on piano.

B flat harmonic minor scale

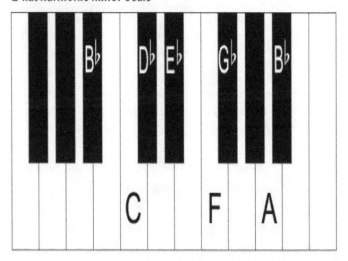

Here's the Bb harmonic minor scale on the treble clef.

B flat harmonic minor scale

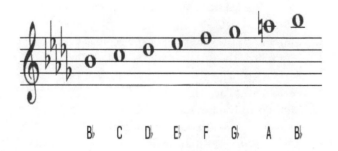

Here's the Bb harmonic minor scale on the bass clef.

B flat harmonic minor scale

B♭ C D♭ E♭ F G♭ A B♭

B Flat Melodic Minor Scale

Let's now learn how to form the B flat melodic minor scale. While the harmonic minor scale raises only the seventh note of the natural minor scale by a half step, the melodic minor scale raises both the sixth and seventh notes by a half step.

The notes of the B flat natural minor scale (as we've seen) are B♭, C, D♭, E♭, F, G♭, A♭, B♭. For the B flat melodic minor scale we raise the 6th and 7th notes by a half step and this results inB♭, C, D♭, E♭, F, G, A, B♭. These notes are used when ascending. When descending, you go back to the natural minor scale.

Notes of the Bb melodic minor scale ascending: B♭, C, D♭, E♭, F, G, A, B♭.

Notes of the Bb melodic minor scale descending: B ♭ , C, D ♭ , E ♭ , F, G ♭ , A ♭ , B ♭ . (These are the notes of the Bb natural minor scale.)

The formula for a melodic minor scale (ascending) is W-H-W-W-W-W-H. The descending formula is the natural minor scale formula backwards.

Melodic B flat Minor Scale Intervals

1. Tonic: The 1st note of the Bb melodic minor scale is Bb.
2. Major 2nd: The 2nd note of the scale is C.
3. Minor 3rd: The 3rd note of the scale is Db.
4. Perfect 4th: The 4th note of the scale is Eb.
5. Perfect 5th: The 5th note is F.
6. Major 6th: The 6th note is G.
7. Major 7th: The 7th note is A.
8. Perfect 8th: The 8th note of the Bb melodic minor scale is Bb.

Here's the B-flat melodic minor scale on piano, ascending.

B flat melodic minor scale (ascending)

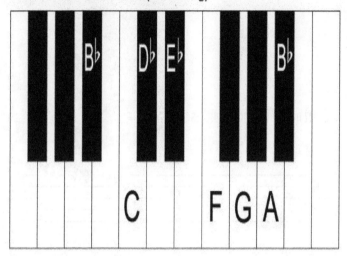

Here's the B flat melodic minor scale on the treble clef.

B flat melodic minor scale ascending

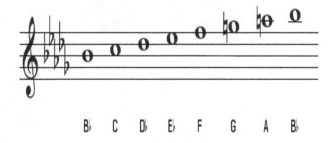

B♭   C   D♭   E♭   F   G   A   B♭

Here's the scale on the bass clef.

B flat melodic minor scale ascending

B♭   C   D♭   E♭   F   G   A   B♭

B Flat Minor Scale

In this lesson, we will learn how to play the B flat minor scale. The three types of minor scales are the natural, melodic and harmonic minor scales. We will take a look at all three of them here.

We will learn the notes, intervals and scale degrees of the B flat minor scale (natural, melodic and harmonic) on the piano, treble and bass clef.

B flat is an enharmonic of A sharp. On piano, the same keys are used to play the two scales. In terms of sound, they are identical. The only difference is the names of the notes. The notes of the A sharp natural minor scale are A♯, B♯, C♯, D♯, E♯, F♯, and G♯.

B Flat Natural Minor Scale

The notes of the B flat natural minor scale are B♭, C, D♭, E♭, F, G♭, and A♭. This scale has 5 flats.

Highly Recommended: Click here for the BEST piano/keyboard course I've come across online.

Let's take a look at the intervals of the Bb minor scale.

Note Intervals:

1. Tonic – The 1st note of the B-flat natural minor scale is Bb.
2. Major 2nd – The 2nd note of the scale is C.
3. Minor 3rd – The 3rd note of the scale is Db.
4. Perfect 4th – The 4th note of the scale is Eb.
5. Perfect 5th – The 5th note of the scale is F.
6. Minor 6th – The 6th note of the scale is Gb.
7. Minor 7th – The 7th note of the scale is Ab.
8. Perfect 8th – The 8th note of the A-flat natural minor scale is Bb.

Here's a diagram of the B flat minor scale on piano/keyboard.

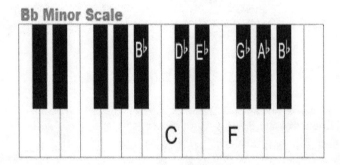

Here's the B flat natural minor scale on the treble clef.

B flat minor scale

Here's the B flat natural minor scale on the bass clef.

B flat minor scale

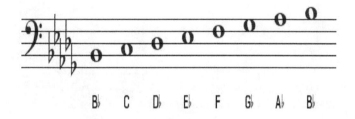

How about the scale degrees? They are as follows:

1. Tonic: Bb
2. Supertonic: C
3. Mediant: Db
4. Subdominant: Eb
5. Dominant: F
6. Submediant: Gb
7. Subtonic: Ab
8. Octave: Bb

There's a formula for forming natural minor scales using whole steps and half steps. That formula is W-H-W-W-H-W-W. "W" stands for whole step and "H" stands for half step.

Let's form the B flat minor scale with this formula. Of course, our starting note is Bb. From Bb, we take a whole step to C. Next, we take a half step to Db. From Db, a whole step takes us to Eb. Another whole step takes us to F. From F, we go up a half step to Gb. From Gb, a whole step takes us to Ab. Finally, the last whole step returns us to Bb.

The relative major key for the key of Bb minor is Db major. A natural minor scale/key consists of the same notes as its relative major. The sixth note of the major scale becomes the root note of its relative minor.

Let's now learn the piano fingerings for the Bb minor scale.

On both the left and right hands, the thumb is finger 1, index finger is finger two, middle finger is finger 3, ring finger is finger 4 and pinky (little) finger is finger 5.

- A Sharp Minor Notes: A♯, B♯, C♯, D♯, E♯, F♯, G♯, A♯
- B Flat Minor Notes: B♭, C, D♭, E♭, F, G♭, A♭, B♭
- Fingerings (Left Hand): 2, 1, 3, 2, 1, 4, 3, 2
- Fingerings (Right Hand): 2, 1, 2, 3, 1, 2, 3, 4

Triad chords in the key of Bb minor and their notes:

1. Chord i – B flat minor. Notes: Bb – Db – F
2. Chord iidim – C diminished. Notes: C – Eb- Gb

3. Chord III – D flat major. Notes: Db – F – Ab
4. Chord iv – E flat minor. Notes: Eb – Gb – Bb
5. Chord v – F minor. Notes: F – Ab – C
6. Chord VI – G flat major. Notes: Gb – Bb – Db
7. Chord VII – A flat major. Notes: Ab – C – Eb

B Flat Harmonic Minor Scale

Now that we know the notes of the B flat minor scale (natural), we now take a look at the B flat harmonic minor scale.

To play a harmonic minor scale, you simply raise the seventh note of the natural minor scale by a half-step as you go up and down the scale. For example, the notes of the natural B flat minor scale are B♭, C, D♭, E♭, F, G♭, A♭, B♭. To form the B flat harmonic minor scale, we raise the seventh note by a half step and this results in B♭, C, D♭, E♭, F, G♭, A, B♭.

The formula for forming a harmonic minor scale is W-H-W-W-H-W 1/2-H. (Whole step – half step – whole step – whole step – half step – whole step and a 1/2 step – half step.)

Harmonic Minor Scale Intervals

1. Tonic: The 1st note of the Bb harmonic minor scale is Bb.
2. Major 2nd: The 2nd note of the scale is C.
3. Minor 3rd: The 3rd note of the scale is Db.
4. Perfect 4th: The 4th note of the scale is Eb.

5. Perfect 5th: The 5th note of the scale is F.
6. Minor 6th: The 6th note of the scale is Gb.
7. Major 7th: The 7th note of the scale is A.
8. Perfect 8th: The 8th note of the Bb harmonic minor scale is Bb.

Here's a diagram of the harmonic B flat minor scale on piano.

B flat harmonic minor scale

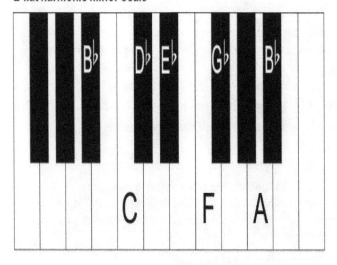

Here's the Bb harmonic minor scale on the treble clef.

B flat harmonic minor scale

B♭　C　D♭　E♭　F　G♭　A　B♭

Here's the Bb harmonic minor scale on the bass clef.

B flat harmonic minor scale

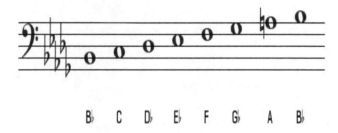

B♭　C　D♭　E♭　F　G♭　A　B♭

B Flat Melodic Minor Scale

Let's now learn how to form the B flat melodic minor scale.
While the harmonic minor scale raises only the seventh
note of the natural minor scale by a half step, the melodic
minor scale raises both the sixth and seventh notes by a
half step.

The notes of the B flat natural minor scale (as we've seen) are B♭, C, D♭, E♭, F, G♭, A♭, B♭. For the B flat melodic minor scale we raise the 6th and 7th notes by a half step and this results inB♭, C, D♭, E♭, F, G, A, B♭. These notes are used when ascending. When descending, you go back to the natural minor scale.

Notes of the Bb melodic minor scale ascending: B♭, C, D♭, E♭, F, G, A, B♭.

Notes of the Bb melodic minor scale descending: B♭, C, D♭, E♭, F, G♭, A♭, B♭. (These are the notes of the Bb natural minor scale.)

The formula for a melodic minor scale (ascending) is W-H-W-W-W-W-H. The descending formula is the natural minor scale formula backwards.

Melodic B flat Minor Scale Intervals

1. Tonic: The 1st note of the Bb melodic minor scale is Bb.
2. Major 2nd: The 2nd note of the scale is C.
3. Minor 3rd: The 3rd note of the scale is Db.
4. Perfect 4th: The 4th note of the scale is Eb.
5. Perfect 5th: The 5th note is F.
6. Major 6th: The 6th note is G.
7. Major 7th: The 7th note is A.
8. Perfect 8th: The 8th note of the Bb melodic minor scale is Bb.

Here's the B-flat melodic minor scale on piano, ascending.

B flat melodic minor scale (ascending)

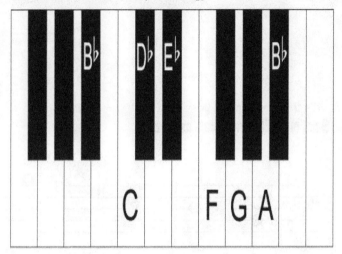

Here's the B flat melodic minor scale on the treble clef.

B flat melodic minor scale ascending

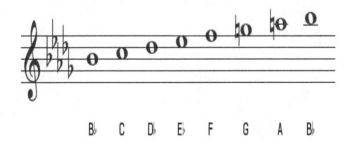

Here's the scale on the bass clef.

B flat melodic minor scale ascending

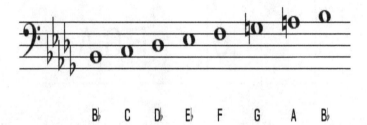

Bb   C   Db   Eb   F   G   A   Bb

B Minor Scale

This lesson is all about the B minor scale. We will take a look at the three types of minor scale, the natural minor, melodic minor and harmonic minor scales.

B Natural Minor Scale

Let's start with the B natural minor scale. This scale consists of the pitches, B, C♯, D, E, F♯, G and A. It has two sharps.

Note Intervals of Bm Scale:

1. Tonic: B is the 1st note of the B natural minor scale.
2. Major 2nd: C# is the 2nd note of the scale.
3. Minor 3rd: D is the 3rd note of the scale.
4. Perfect 4th: E is the 4th note of the scale.
5. Perfect 5th: F# is the 5th note of the scale.
6. Minor 6th: G is the 6th note of the scale.
7. Minor 7th: A is the 7th note of the scale.
8. Perfect 8th: B (one octave higher) is the 8th note of the B natural minor scale.

Here's a diagram of the B minor scale (Bm scale) on the treble clef.

B Minor Scale (Treble Clef)

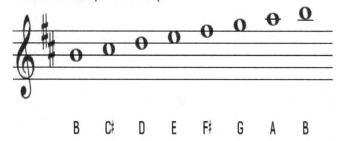

B   C♯   D   E   F♯   G   A   B

Here's the B minor scale on the bass clef.

B Minor Scale (Bass Clef)

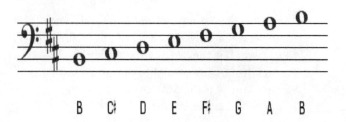

B   C♯   D   E   F♯   G   A   B

Here's the B minor scale on piano.

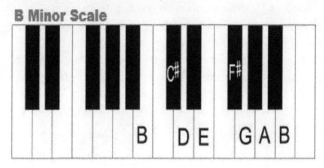

Scale Degrees:

1. Tonic: B
2. Supertonic: C#
3. Mediant: D
4. Subdominant: E
5. Dominant: F#
6. Submediant: G
7. Subtonic: A
8. Octave: B

The relative major of B minor is D major. Minor keys and their relative major make use of the same notes. The notes of the B minor scale as we've seen are B, C♯, D, E, F♯, G, and A. For the D major scale, it's D, E, F♯, G, A, B and C♯. The difference is the root note of the two scales. The sixth note of a major scale becomes the root note of its relative minor.

You can memorize this formula to form any natural minor scale: whole step – half step – whole step – whole step – half step – whole step – whole step or w – h – w – w – h – w

– w. (A whole step skips a key while a half step moves to the next key.) Let's try this with the B minor scale. Let's start on B and move a whole step to C#. From C# move a half step to D. Next, we move a whole step from D to E. From E, let's move a whole step to F#. Next, we go up a half step from F# to G. From G, we move up one whole step to A. Finally, we move a whole step from A to B.

What are the fingerings for the B minor scale? They are as follows:

- Notes: B, C#, D, E, F#, G, A, B
- Fingerings (Left Hand): 4, 3, 2, 1, 4, 3, 2, 1
- Fingerings (Right Hand): 1, 2, 3, 1, 2, 3, 4, 5

Thumb: 1, index finger: 2, middle finger: 3, ring finger: 4 and pinky finger: 5.

Let's now take a look at the chords in the key of B minor.

1. Chord i: B minor. Its notes are B – D – F#.
2. Chord ii: C# diminished. Its notes are C# – E – G.
3. Chord III: D major. Its notes are D – F# – A.
4. Chord iv: E minor. Its notes are E – G – B.
5. Chord v: F# minor. Its notes are F# – A – C#.
6. Chord VI: G major. Its notes are G – B – D.
7. Chord VII: A major. Its notes are A – C# – E.

B Harmonic Minor Scale

Let's now take a look at the B harmonic minor scale.

The harmonic minor scale raises the seventh note of the natural minor scale by a half-step, when ascending and descending the scale. For example, the notes of the B natural minor scale are B – C♯ – D – E – F♯ – G – A – B. For the B harmonic minor scale, the notes are B – C♯ – D – E – F♯ – G – A# – B. The seventh note of the scale has been changed from A to A#. It's now a half step (or semitone) higher.

The formula for forming a harmonic minor scale is W-H-W-W-H-W 1/2-H.

Harmonic Minor Scale Intervals:

1. Tonic: The 1st note of the B harmonic minor scale is B.
2. Major 2nd: The 2nd note of the scale is C#.
3. Minor 3rd: The 3rd note of the scale is D.
4. Perfect 4th: The 4th note of the scale is E.
5. 5. Perfect 5th: The 5th note of the scale is F#.
6. 6. Minor 6th: The 6th note of the scale is G.
7. 7. Major 7th: The 7th note of the scale is A#.
8. 8. Perfect 8th: The 8th note of the scale is B.

B harmonic minor scale on piano.

B Harmonic Minor Scale

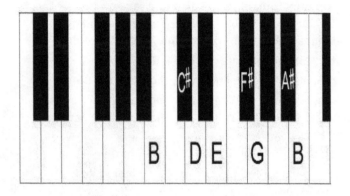

Here's the B harmonic minor scale on the treble clef.

B harmonic minor scale

B C♯ D E F♯ G A♯ B

Here's the B harmonic minor scale on the bass clef.

B harmonic minor scale

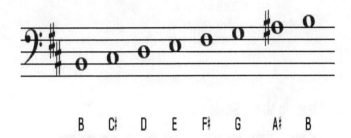

B   C#   D   E   F#   G   A#   B

B Melodic Minor Scale

Let's now take a look at the melodic minor scale. For this scale, you raise the sixth and seventh notes by a half step as you go up the scale and then return to the natural minor as you go down the scale. The notes of the B melodic minor scale ascending are: B – C# – D – E – F# – G# – A# – B. The notes of the B melodic minor scale descending are: B – C# – D – E – F# – G – A – B.

The formula for a melodic minor scale is W-H-W-W-W-W-H. The descending formula is the natural minor scale formula backwards.

Melodic B Minor Scale Intervals

1. Tonic: The 1st note of the B melodic minor scale is B.
2. Major 2nd: The 2nd note of the scale is C#.

3. Minor 3rd: The 3rd is D.
4. Perfect 4th: The 4th note is E.
5. Perfect 5th: The 5th note is F#.
6. Major 6th: The 6th is G#.
7. Major 7th: The 7th is A#.
8. Perfect 8th: The 8th note of the scale is B.

B Minor Scale (Melodic) on Piano:

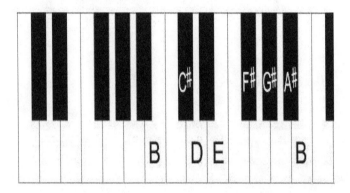

Here's the scale on the treble clef.

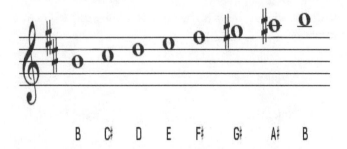

Here's the scale on the bass clef.

B melodic minor scale

B   C♯   D   E   F♯   G♯   A♯   B

Remember that for the melodic minor scale, when descending, you play the natural minor scale.

The Sharp Sign: ♯

Let's learn about the sharp sign. This is the actual symbol: ♯. However in type, it is often written like this: # (same symbol as pound, number sign or hash symbol on social media.)

The main difference between the actual sharp sign and the pound (number) or hash sign is that the number/hashtag sign has two horizontal strokes while the sharp musical sign has two slanted parallel lines which rise from left to right, in order to avoid being obscured by the horizontal musical staff lines.

Highly Recommended: Click here for one of the BEST piano/keyboard courses I've seen online.

A sharp symbol, when placed in front a note, increases its pitch by a half step or semitone. For instance, C♯ is a half step higher than C, and D♯ is a half step higher than D.

A SHARP SIGN

On piano, the black keys are usually referred to as sharp or flat keys. For example, the key to the immediate right of C is C♯, the key to the immediate right of D is D♯ and the key to the immediate right of F is F♯. As we mentioned earlier, they are a half step higher than the keys to their left.

Since they are a half step lower than the keys to their right they can also be called flats. **Flat symbol:** ♭ . The term for this is enharmonics. Enharmonics are notes that are the same pitch but are known by two different names, for instance C-sharp and D-flat. So, C sharp is an enharmonic of D flat. But on piano, they make use of the same key. The same key is labeled C sharp and D flat, the same key is labeled A flat and G flat, and so on. (But for the purpose of this lesson our main focus is sharps.)

Sharp Sign   Number Sign

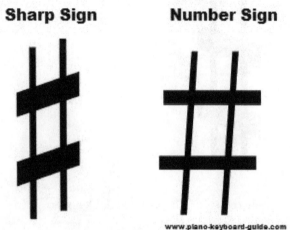

While the black keys are called sharp or flat keys, the white ones are called natural keys.

In terms of sharp and natural keys, the 12 keys on piano starting from C are C, C♯, D, D♯, E, F, F♯, G, G♯, A, A♯, and B. C, D, E, F, G, A and B are the natural keys, while C♯, D♯, F♯, G♯ and A♯ are obviously, the sharps.

Here's a diagram showing sharps and natural keys on your piano:

SHARPS AND NATURAL KEYS ON PIANO

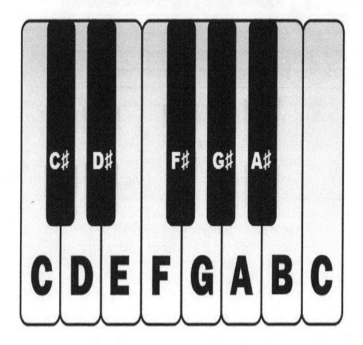

In fact, the sharp symbol before a note in a musical piece simply means to play the next key to the right, whether it's a black key or a white key. When a sharp (♯) symbol appears before a note, it applies to that note for the rest of the measure. Once the measure ends, the sharp is no longer in effect. To cancel out sharp in a measure, a natural sign is used.

G Major Key Signature

Someti mes, the sharp symbol is stated in the key signature. One example is the G key signature. This is because there is one sharp in the G major scale called F#. (The G major scale's pitches are G-A-B-C-D-E-F#.) That way there is no need to place a sharp before each and every F note. Every time you see an F, for the entire piece, it's actually F sharp that must be played on your piano. If a sharp (or flat) sign is not stated in the key signature but only on a certain place in a musical piece, it is called an accidental.

Having said all of this, I have to make one thing clear. This is the fact that sharps and flats are not black keys. All black keys are either sharp or flat but not all sharps and flats are black keys. White keys can be sharp or flat too. For example, on a piece of music, if you see a sharp on the note E, it means to play the note to the right of E on your piano. It means to play the key that is a semitone higher. This is actually, the note E#, although it is normally labeled as F on your piano and is the same key. E# and F are enharmonics. For a better understanding of this read the difference between notes and keys on the piano.

To draw a sharp sign, slant the horizontal lines of the sign upwards and to the right. The space in the middle of the sharp sign is placed on the same staff line or space as the notehead that follows it. The height of the sharp sign is about three staff spaces.

Sharp & Double Sharp Sign

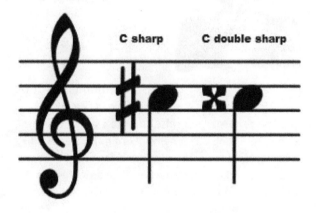

Double Sharp Sign

A DOUBLE SHARP SIGN

Another musical symbol is the double sharp. A double-sharp is the equivalent of two sharps, and raises a note's pitch by two semitones (a whole tone). This symbol is similar to a bold x, and is placed before a note like other accidentals. Its height is one staff space, and it is centered on the same line or space as the notehead that it alters. A double sharp simply means to play the note that is two semitones higher. So for instance, if you see this symbol before the note C on a musical piece, you would have to play D on your piano. As a beginner, you don't have to bother with this too much as yet. This sign is not as common as regular sharps and flats.

Natural Sign: ♮

Let's learn about the natural sign (♮).

We have already looked at the other accidental signs, namely sharp signs and flat signs. In a nutshell, a flat sign before a note means that its pitch should be lowered by a half step or semitone, while a sharp sign indicates that the pitch should be raised by a half step or semitone.

A natural is an accidental which cancels previous accidentals. For instance, let's say a previous note in a piece of music is Bb, if a natural symbol precedes the new note, you are to play B. To explain this further, the key of G has one sharp, F#. To indicate that the note, F should be played and not F#, a natural sign will be placed before the note.

Other examples:

If a note is in D sharp, a natural symbol will bring the note back to its natural tone which is D. If a note is in E flat, a natural will bring it back to its natural tone which is E.

What a Natural Sign Looks Like (How to Draw)

So what does this sign look like? Here we go: ♮. It looks almost like a sharp sign, but some of its lines are not as long. The space in the middle of this sign is placed on the exact line or space as the notehead it affects. Its height is about three staff spaces.

Natural Sign

F Natural (Natural Note)

When the measure ends, the natural, like other accidentals, no longer has any effect. It is canceled by the bar line. In the subsequent measure you are to resort to the note that the key signature indicates. For instance, in the key of F, which has one flat, Bb, if a natural sign precedes the note B, you have to play B for the rest of the measure. But when a new measure starts, you are to start playing Bb once again.

How about if one wants to cancel out a double sharp or double flat? It is acceptable to write a single natural. Two naturals (♮♮) can be written as well, but a single one is normally used.

NATURAL KEYS ON PIANO

A note is natural when it is neither flat not sharp (nor double-flat or double-sharp). White piano keys are called naturals. There are seven of them, namely, C-D-E-F-G-A-B. After B, the next natural note is C and it continues with the same pattern. These 7 notes make up the C major scale, sometimes regarded as the natural major scale because all its note are natural, whereas every other major scale has at least one sharp or flat.

When you come across a natural sign in a piece of music, the key to be played will always be a white one, unlike sharps and flats which can be black or white.

The Flat Sign: ♭

Let's take a look at the flat sign. When typing, we normally use the regular lowercase letter, "b" to represent this sign, but the actual symbol is ♭ which is is a stylized lowercase "b".

In terms of its effect on a note, this sign is basically the opposite of a sharp sign. When you come across a sharp before a note on a musical piece, it means to play the note one half step (semitone) higher. When you come across a flat sign, you are to play the note that is a semitone lower. For instance B♭ is a semitone lower than B. B♭ is the black key to the immediate left of B on your piano. E♭ is one semitone (half step) lower than E and is the key to the immediate left of E on your piano. A♭ is one semitone lower than A, and so on. Anytime you see a flat symbol before any note on a piece, go one piano key to the left.

FLAT
SIGN

The black keys on your piano can be either sharp or flat. It depends on the **key signature** of the music and the choice of the composer. Each black key is usually represented by two note names, but in theory, they can have other names (as we shall talk about later).

Examples of keys having two names: The key to the right of C can be called C#, but since it is to the left of D, it can be called Db as well. The key to the right of D can be called D# but since it is to the left of E it can be called E flat as well. In other words, one half step higher makes a key sharp, while a half step lower makes it flat.

Enharmonics are notes that are the same pitch but are known by at least two different names. C sharp and D flat are enharmonics of each other. The same can be said of D sharp and E flat, G sharp and A flat, F sharp and G flat, and A sharp and B flat.

The white keys are called natural keys.

In terms of natural keys and flats, the 12 keys on your piano in order, starting on C natural are C, D♭, D, E♭, E, F, G♭, G, A♭, A, B♭ and B.

Here's a diagram showing natural and flat keys on piano.

FLATS AND NATURAL KEYS ON PIANO

Having said all of this, allow me to sound a note of caution. Notes and keys are not the same. Beginners are usually of the view that flats and sharps are only played on black keys. This is not so. A flat sign means to play the key that is a half step lower, therefore if you come across an F note on a piece of music, it means to play the note that is a half step lower. That note is F flat and it is the enharmonic of E on piano, a white key. If you see a C flat, it means to play one half step lower than C which is a white key on your piano, the enharmonic of B.Learn why notes and keys are not the same here.

When you come across a flat note on a musical piece, you are to assume that the note will stay flat for the rest of that measure. It is not necessary for a flat sign to be placed before that note again until the measure ends. When the measure ends, the flat is no longer in effect. The same applies to the other type of accidentals, known as sharps. To cancel out an accidental (sharp or flat), a **natural sign** is used.

F Major Key Signature

Someti
mes, the flat note is placed in the key signature. For
example, the key of F major has one flat, Bb. The pitches for
the F major scale are F-G-A-Bb-C-D-E. Every time you come
across B, you are supposed to play Bb. Every B is flatted in
the key of F, unless it's canceled out by a natural sign.
Thanks to key signatures which indicate which notes have
to be flattered or sharpened, you don't have to keep using
accidentals throughout a piece of written music. This makes

everything cleaner and simpler.

Flat & Double Flat Sign

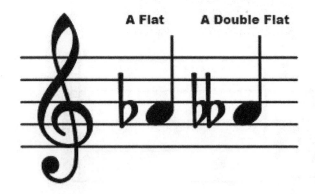

How does one draw a flat sign?

A flat musical sign consists of a small loop and a stem. It is placed in front the note. The loop is placed directly on the line or space of the notehead to which it belongs. If the flat effects a pitch that is on a space, the loop should be in the middle of that space. If the notehead is on a line, the line should run through the middle of the loop of the flat sign. The stem of the flat sign is about two and a half staff spaces in length.

**Double
Flat
Sign**

Double Flat Sign

Another musical symbol is the double-flat. Double flats lower a note by two half steps (a whole step). For example, a double flat symbol before E means to play the key that is two semitones lower on your piano; that key is D. This symbol consists of two flat signs next to each other, touching each other. The double-flat symbol is not as common.

How to Play Chromatic Scale on Piano

The chromatic scale is arguably one of the easiest scales to understand, particularly on piano. This is because you simply go from one key to the other without skipping any. This scale consists of 12 notes, each a half step (semitone) apart.

My Best Recommendation: Click here for the BEST piano/keyboard course I've seen on the Internet.

For instance, let's say you start on the note C. The C chromatic scale would consist of the notes, C, C#, D, D#, E, F, F#, G, G#,A, A# and B. Since you started on C, you can end on C. But these are the 12 notes that make up the scale. As you go down you play the same keys, except that some of the notes would be enharmonic equivalents, which means that they are the same keys with different names. The notes played in descending order can be called C, B, A, Ab, G, Gb, F, E, Eb, D,Db and C. Normally, as you go up, some of the notes are sharped and as you go down, some of the notes are flatted.

CHROMATIC SCALE

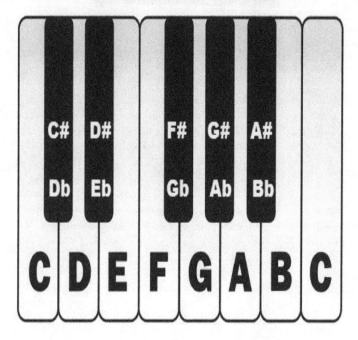

How about starting on the note, D (for instance)? It's basically the same thing. All you do is move from one key to the next. Starting on the note D, to form this scale, the 12 notes of the scale are D, D#, E, F, F#, G, G#, A, A#, B, C and C#.

The formula for this scale is very simple: All notes are included. In the key of C, you start on C and end on C. In the key of G, you start on G and end on G. And so on.

How about the fingering for this scale? What fingers go on what keys? Let's find out.

Only three fingers are used to play the scale. They are the thumb (1st finger), index finger (2nd finger) and middle finger (third finger).

How to Play Chromatic Scale on Piano with Right Hand

Chromatic Scale Fingering (Right Hand)

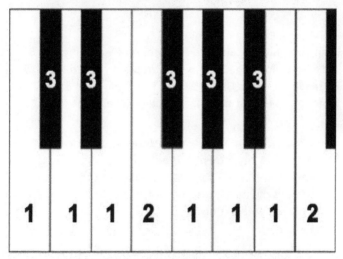

1: Thumb, 2: index finger, 3: middle finger

Starting on the note, C, going up the scale, the fingering for the right hand is 1313 123 1313 12. Starting on the note C, going down the scale, the fingering for the right hand is simply reversed. Descending, the fingering is 21 3131 321 3131.

In other words, starting on C, ascending, the 1st finger (or thumb) plays C, 3rd finger plays C#, 1st finger plays D and 3rd plays D#. 1st finger plays E, 2nd plays F and 3rd plays F#. 1st finger plays G, 3rd plays G#, 1st finger plays A and 3rd plays A#. Then 1st finger plays B and 2nd plays C.

Going down the scale, 2nd finger plays C and 1st plays B. 3rd finger plays Bb, 1st plays A, 3rd plays Ab and 1st plays G. 3rd finger plays Gb, 2nd plays F and 1st plays E. 3rd finger plays Eb, 1st plays D, 3rd plays Db and 1st plays C.

When ascending, any time a white key immediately follows another white key, you play it with the second finger. When descending, if a white key follows another, the first one is played with the 2nd finger, while the one to its immediate left is played with 1st finger.

All the black keys are played with the middle (third) finger.

Here's a video I made which shows how to play this scale with the right and left hand.

How to Play Chromatic Scale on Piano with Left Hand

How about the left hand?

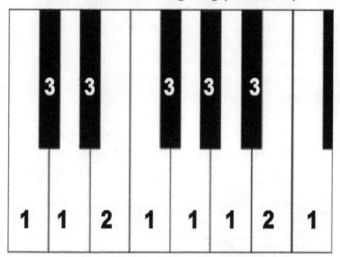

Chromatic Scale Fingering (Left Hand)

1: Thumb, 2: index finger, 3: middle finger

After you have mastered the right hand fairly well, you can move to the left hand. Starting on C, the fingering for the left hand is 1313 213 1313 21, ascending. To go down the scale, you simply reverse the order of numbers. The same fingers play the same keys. So descending, the fingering is 12 3131 312 3131.

Starting on C, the 1st finger (thumb) plays C, 3rd finger plays C#, 1st finger plays D and 3rd finger plays D#. Since we have one white note immediately following another, we use the 2nd finger to play E, 1st finger plays F and 3rd finger plays F#. 1st finger plays G, 3rd finger plays G#, 1st finger plays A, and 3rd finger plays A#. A white note follows another white note once again, so you should use the 2nd finger to play B and 1st finger to play C.

To go down the scale, simply play everything in reverse using the same fingers for the same keys. 1st finger plays C and 2nd finger plays B. 3rd finger plays Bb, 1st finger plays A, 3rd finger plays Ab and 1st plays G. 3rd finger plays Gb, 1st plays F and 2nd plays E. 3rd plays Eb, 1st plays D, 3rd plays Db and 1st plays C.

As is the case with the right hand, for the left hand, all the black keys are played with the middle (third) finger.

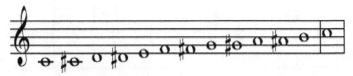

The chromatic scale, ascending

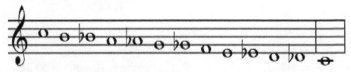

The chromatic scale, descending

The chromatic scale, ascending

The chromatic scale, descending

Here's the chromatic scale, ascending and descending. In terms of the note names that can be used (or enharmonics), these are only examples and can vary.

This scale has no set spelling agreed upon by all. Its spelling is, however, often dependent upon major or minor key signatures and whether the scale is ascending or descending.

Learn How To Play Piano & Keyboard

Do you want to learn how to play piano? If so, you're in the right place. Our piano lesson reviews will guide you into choosing the best courses available online. You will find reviews of the best programs right here. Find out what we deem to be the top piano courses on the Internet.

I have bought several online piano courses for testing purposes and after checking them out thoroughly, have narrowed them down to the ones I think are best. I make recommendations having personally tried these piano lessons. What is my top recommendation for learning how to play piano?

If you are to purchase just ONE course from the Internet, the one I recommend is Pianoforall. Unlike other courses that give students false hope, this one really delivers. The folks at PianoForAll keep the promises made on their site. To begin with, their promises are realistic. I recommend their lessons highly.

Many online piano lessons have failed due to the fact that they place too much stress on the technical aspects of learning to play. Some courses make learning how to play piano and keyboard so tedious and boring, it's unbelievable! Pianoforall is different. It's clear that its creator, Robin Hall understands exactly what is necessary to start playing piano and keyboards quickly and easily.

Pianoforall piano lessons include as many as 10 ebooks, 500 audio and 200 videos. I like the way the lessons are laid out, taking you step by step. The entire process motivates you to learn piano.

This course is different to other courses in that it doesn't focus on too much abstract theory. Clearly, the traditional methods of teaching have not worked for most piano students. Boring methods have caused many people to give up on the piano. In my estimation, Pianoforall is a much more fun way to learn. While these lessons are challenging, it's a more student friendly approach.

As for the price, it's worth every cent. You can easily spend several times the amount on hiring a piano teacher, whether with a group or on your own, and end up being dissatisfied. Compared to other piano lessons that cost the same, this one is unmatched.

Apart from having thoroughly examined Pianoforall, I have read several positive reviews about it online and have gotten great feedback from users. I'd like to encourage you to check it out for yourself. Visit the Piano4all site and learn more about it.

(Look at eBook or write an email to lecasedivetulonia@gmail.com to have the link.)

Printed in the USA
CPSIA information can be obtained
at www.ICGtesting.com
LVHW101640040124
768175LV00009B/296